Bless Me Indeed

Discover the secret of Success;
through the power of a prayer that can bring
supernatural blessings to your life

JANET KISYOMBE

Ordering Information:

For orders and inquiries, please contact:
1-888-375-9818
www.toplinkpublishing.com
bookorder@toplinkpublishing.com

Printed in the United States of America

CONTENTS

1 Chronicles 4: 9-10: Jabez cried to the God of Israel saying
"Oh, that you will BLESS ME INDEED.
And ENLARGE MY BORDERS.
And that your HAND MIGHT BE with me.
And you will keep me from evil so that it might not
hurt me!"
And God Granted His Request.

ACKNOWLEDGMENT

This book is dedicated to my late grandparents, Mr. Job Robinson Kisyombe and Mrs. Elise (Nalwanda) Kisyombe. I wish you were here today to celebrate this victory with me. I am so blessed because of the good and Godly seed you planted in me while you were still living on this planet earth. Rest in peace my beloved until we will meet again.

I am a daughter of an amazing woman, a life fighter, and a single mother--Dr. Victoria Kisyombe. I say thank you mama for your nonstop endless love, prayers, and support. I am also a proud sister to Daniel, Dr. Nai, Dr. Ludovick, Linda, and Noel. I am a proud mother to a wonderful, amazing son, Moses. My baba - Mr. Lembrise Kipuyo, my uncles, Michael Simwaba, Gamaliel Kisyombe thank you for believing in me since I was just a young girl. To all my Kisyombe's family members and Professor Minga's family - I am who I am today because of your nonstop love and prayers.

I give many thanks to you, my friends, Mr. Kenneth Kasigila, Viva Masebo, and Christabel Ngowi , for seeing the potential in me and encouraging me to pursue my dream. To my Godly- given best girlfriends: Robby Kikaro, Lilian Mtei, Margreth Mwenda, Oliver Ngole, Sekela Polisya, Vanilla Mgeni, Rona Lyimo, and many others; you are the definition of a true unbroken friendship. Your unconditional love and support have made me who I am today. Without forgetting all my beautiful dialysis world co-workers and my patients, I give you nothing more than a huge hug and love.

Much gratitude goes to you my newfound friends and family members at the Toplink Publishing Company. The full team working on this book to ensure its success and its go global mission; Jeff Keller, Eugene Gutierrez, Cheryl Brent and many others. Susie Igogo, you are an inspiration, thank you so much for believing in my work, and now we have a completely amazing book. I am forever grateful and God bless you all tremendously.

Kijitonyama Lutheran Church continues to do amazing work of God, you are the best. You cannot talk about Kijitonyama without including Mama Nancy Buchcuski. I love you; your name represents the true meaning of love without boundaries.

I call myself blessed because I am surrounded by many wonderful people.

PREFACE

To my dear new best friends, my readers, I want to thank you in advance for your support. I am praying that you will be blessed abundantly indeed by what is written inside this book. By picking and reading this material, I guarantee you that something will shift within you, and you will change for the better as I am a proof witness of that miracle. I am here today to share the wonderful news of the **PRAYER OF JABEZ**, which is believed to have changed many people's lives. And yet, it came to my attention that there are many people who are still not aware of this short, simple, right to the point, but powerful prayer.

The Jabez's story is one of the shortest stories written in the Holy Scripture and yet again, it is one of the most famous and powerful miraculous prayer found in the Bible. I am very excited to share this wonderful news with you. The prayer of Jabez combined with my voracious habit of listening to God's word and Bible's teachings has changed me a lot. Now I view life with a positive attitude knowing that the only thing that is stopping me is me, myself, and I only.

I will be a foolish and not a very good Christian if I don't share this wonderful news with you. I personally give credit to the prayer of Jabez since it has helped me to step out of my comfort zone, step out of my daily routine, and start writing this book. As a result, today, I am able to share my passion with you. I have to say I have found joy in writing this material, which I know will be of great substance to many others. It humbles me and gives me a feeling of satisfaction to know that I am doing a great deed to someone else. This is my way of paying it forward.

This book is written in a very plain and easy to understand English language so that it can be readable and relatable to all the readers from different walks of life. The main purpose of writing this book is to bless you (aside from me) and to start living a life of more than enough and start living an abundant life that God has intended for you to have.

I am hoping the work of this publication will lift up your spirit and give you a feeling of anticipation. I am praying that this book will give you the spiritual guidance to start receiving and living in God's full benediction. This work alone will show you that it is very possible to change your life today from a life of lack and limitation, to a life of more than enough, a life full of God's abundance. Also, it is within my intention that you will gain cognition and insights about Bible teachings, in regards to experiencing the total package of God's complete favor and protections.

Lastly, I will advise you that during your reading, apart from paying attention to the prayer of Jabez itself, keep in mind the two verses which are written below. In combination with a prayer of Jabez, use them as a foundation to help you to fully absorb all the teachings of God that have been revealed to you.

Hosea 4:6 says, "My people are destroyed for lack of knowledge." Reject this to be the hindrance to your success. Jesus is giving us another tool to use while opening the secret box to God's richness. On Matthew 7:7 - Jesus is instructing us to Ask, Seek and Knock. He says, "Ask and it will be given to you; seek and you will find; knock and the door will be opened to you." Believe me when I say that this is all the major secret there is. Later on, we will dive deep into this as we keep on exploring God's word.

I pray today that mediocrity, poverty, and lack of limitations are not going to be the case for you. You are not going to perish just because you lack the facts about God's kingdom. And surely, you are not going to live a life of less than enough and full of struggles just because you didn't hear good news about the abundance and provision that you are entitled to receive from God. Today, we ask for God to Bless Us all Indeed.

Be blessed and enjoy reading as I have enjoyed writing this book. I love you all.

Yours truly
Janet Job Kisyombe

INTRODUCTION

My Personal Encounter with Jabez

In my past years, I have encountered a lot of hardships. I had hoped for my journey to be a smooth ride, but it wasn't. In almost every area, I hit rock bottom physically, emotionally, mentally, and even professionally. I do believe this is not my song only because I might be singing someone else's song as well. Life for most of us is all about ups and downs, highs and lows, hills and valleys.

Through all my struggles, I had no option except to turn to God for answers. I am lucky to be born in a good family of Christians. For most of my childhood, I have to say that I was raised well by my Christian grandparents. Since I could remember, God has been the center of everything under my grandfather's roof. As I struggle to find answers, I tend to turn to the good book – the Bible – for solutions and try to find a meaning of my existence. Also, I try to find ways to turn my life around for a better living. One thing I know for certain is that God has not intended me to live a tough, mediocre life for the rest of my life. I am sure that there is something within me that is very special and very different. I have never accepted poverty to be my norm; I believe we all can carve our own fate.

I am now taking you back during one winter season few years past. I remember vividly that it was very cold outside. When looking outdoors, all you see was this white smoke coming from the chimneys of most houses. I reside in a beautiful small town of Owings Mills. The place is rich of small hills covered by beautiful trees. To say the weather is always unpredictable here in Maryland is an understatement.

One day, I was watching TV, sitting on my sofa in my cozy warm living room, sipping a cup of hot herbal tea. My love for tea is one of my many small luxuries that I enjoy. It does not take much to impress me. I have never been a big fan of coffee, I drink it but not as much as my favorite sweet hot tea with a tint of lemon. With the cold I was feeling, all I needed was a cup of tea and a remote control.

This particular day was one of the few days I had off work. Without having any major plans, I decided to calmly remain in the house and just mind my own business. Normally, when it is cold or during snow time, I tend to take it easy, stay indoors, cuddle myself with a warm blanket, and just try to unwind. Sitting quietly with nothing much to do, just mindless, I switched on my television and switched to a Christian channel; I do not remember exactly which channel it was. One of my favorite shows came on - *Sid Roth's its supernatural show.* You might have seen this show on Christian television channels or on the internet. On each show, there's one guest speaker who comes to talk or witness God's supernatural events that they have witnessed themselves, or miracles that have happened to someone else.

On this very particular day, a man named Gary Keesee was the main guest speaker. In short, the show went on to say that Gary Keesee was so hopelessly in debt to a point that he was even afraid to leave his house. Then God downloaded to him the mysteries of money (yes, you've read it right). Since then, he has gotten out of debt and has taught thousands of people on how to turn their lives around. The good thing about him is that he is a believer in God. Currently, Gary is a millionaire and has taught thousands of people what God showed him.

As a dreamer and a reality chaser, I have been looking for ways to improve my own life. I am a believer in God and I just witnessed on TV about the man who is a believer like me — telling me that the answers to my financial issues can be found in the Bible. The same Bible that I have been exposed to by my mother and my grandparents almost all my life. Gary got my attention! You can just imagine how curious I became to know more – I grabbed a pen and a paper and wrote down his name so I could go back to the only encyclopedia most of us know — *Google*. I typed his name in curiosity and was blown away by what I found.

I was really moved by both Gary Keesee and his wife, Drenda, story. That God has literally turned their lives around, from being poor to being millionaires at present. He stressed out that they solved most of their financial issues by applying the principles of the Bible. Gary and his wife paid cash for their house and cars in two years' time. I said to myself, *"Oh wow, this is what I would like to do myself."* At this point, he seriously captured my attention and without any hesitations, I bought his teaching materials.

Their story sounded more like my struggling story. I have been working so hard, but I just couldn't seem to catch a break. I prayed all kinds of prayers. I sometimes even grab my notebook and start writing down my prayers. I became more determined to turn my life around by using God's wisdom. To cut the story short, through my journey of reading different books and on my daily Bible readings, that's when I came across the prayer of Jabez. For some unknown reasons, I had never heard of Jabez before.

While I was reading Jabez's prayer, one line literally made me pause, and that line simply states - "*And God Answered His request.*" It has been in my habit that when I come across something very interesting, I always want to do some more research, read, and learn more. The same was for Jabez. I had to go back and dig deep about him. Once you write the prayer of Jabez or just the keyword 'Jabez' — different materials written by a man named Bruce Wilkinson will come up. Bruce Wilkinson is the man who literally introduced Jabez to our generation today.

My New Obsession

Now at this point, I decided to make Jabez my new best friend and his prayer as my new obsession. It says in the Bible that God answered Jabez's prayer. Wait a minute now, I asked myself: If God answered Jabez's prayer, then He has to answer my prayers as well. I was so surprised that it took me this long to know about him. I spoke to a couple of people about Jabez and to my amazement, I discovered that there are still many people who do not know anything about his prayer at all. Well, the Bible wrote a little about him, but I am sure it's the substance that counts.

I pulled my laptop again – just between you and me, I just want you to know that my Laptop is my best friend. I have named my laptop my close partner because I spend a lot of my time with it. I sometimes wonder what I will do without it.

I went on and typed the whole prayer and printed several copies just for my references. I have one prayer hanged on my bathroom mirror and I placed another copy in my car compartment. The whole point of having multiple copies printed out was very simple: I just wanted to make sure that I will be able to read the lines over and over again before I even start my day, or before I get to work. I made sure that the four lines of Jabez's prayer are engraved deep down in my unconscious mind.

I made it a personal mission to start talking about Jabez's prayer to my friends and family members. Hence, I am indeed grateful that God has given me this apprehension that I am sharing with you. I am thankful for the provision of tools and means that are making it possible for me to broadcast to a mass number of people. God blesses us with dreams. I am grateful that He has blessed me today with the dream of writing this inspirational and motivational book. When dreams are given to us, it is up to us to act upon our dreams and transform things into a reality.

I have to admit to you that I am not very good at praying. But I can read and I can recite these four lines that Jabez prayed to God. My fellow believers, if God granted Jabez's request by just praying those few lines, I strongly believe that He will listen to us as well. We worship the same God today, God of Israel – God of Abraham, Isaac, and Jacob. He is the same God yesterday, today and tomorrow. His miracles are everywhere even to this very minute. He is the God of compassion. Our sincerity is all that matters.

Now, let us start together by exploring the prayer of Jabez in details. Let us be of open-minded and be ready to receive His blessings with open arms.

You will notice that I have also included several lines from the Bible. I have purposely done so just to help you understand the blessings of God in a whole, and also to fully grasp the fact that God's intention is to bless you so that you can live in His divine provision. The prayer of Jabez will lift your hope in discovering the promises of God that are given to you. It will empower you to boldly face your daily struggles of life and to come to an understanding that nothing is impossible when you ask Him for help.

CHAPTER ONE

Meet Jabez – Who is Jabez?

Jabez cried to the Lord of Israel saying:
'Oh that you will BLESS ME INDEED.
And ENLARGE MY BORDERS.
And that your HAND MIGHT BE with me.
And you will keep me from evil so that it might not hurt me!'
And God Granted His Request."

In most chapters of this book, we will start by reading the four lines that Jabez prayed to God of Israel. The main purpose of doing this is very simple – to ensure that you are opening a chapter with a prayer, at the same time, you are re-reading these four lines over and over again so that this same prayer will be engraved deep down in your unconscious mind. God answered Jabez's prayer, and I am praying today that God will answer all your prayers in Jesus' name.

In this chapter, it is best to learn and explore in depth about the mysterious man named Jabez – who is the main character of our book. The Wikipedia mentions Jabez as a *Biblical figure* whereas in 1 Chronicles Jabez is mentioned as a *well-respected man coming from the Tribe of Judah in the lines of Kings* whose prayer to God was answered.

Strange enough, Jabez is only mentioned twice in the Bible. We first see the name Jabez mentioned in 1 Chronicles 2:55 – but to my understanding here, Jabez is mentioned as a place of origin (city/town), and I am not certain if there is any correlation with Jabez, the person.

1 Chronicles 2:55. "The families of scribes who lived at Jabez were the Tirathites, the Shimeathites and the Sucathites. Those are the Kenites who came from Hammath, the father of the house of Rechab".

Having said that, Jabez's name as a person has only been mentioned in two verses of the Bible. We first find Jabez our book character in 1 Chronicles 4:9 which says that:

"Jabez was more honorable than his brothers.
His mother had named him Jabez, saying,
I gave birth to him in pain."

In short, the name Jabez means *pain, sorrow maker*. Not a good name to name your child at all. You won't be doing your poor child justice if you go and give them the name *Jabez*. This poor baby will be teased every day by his peers by being called 'Pain.' The definition of pain is suffering, agony, torture, torment, discomfort. Not a good name at all levels. Torture and agony was Jabez's name, and he had to bear and live with that name for the rest of his life.

1 Chronicles 4:10

We also find the name Jabez mentioned for the second time at 1 Chronicles 4:10, where the prayer that he prayed to God is being displayed, and this is the same prayer that famously made him a talk of many generations to come.

"Jabez cried out to the God of Israel, "Oh that you would bless me indeed and enlarge my territory! Let your hand be with me, and keep me from harm so that I will be free from pain."

And God granted his request.

I don't know about you, but I get chills each and every time I get to read the last line, which says, "<u>And God granted his request</u>."

I have to pause here and praise God for His kindness, His love which endures forever, and praise Him for His merciful love over our lives. God is wonderful indeed. I pray today that God will grant all your wishes in Jesus Name. We believe and receive His blessings.

To be honest with you, I am not a big fan of 1 Chronicles – My head was spinning when I was reading this book. This chapter is full of weird and hard to pronounce names. The Author of this book is believed to be Ezra – and I think the purpose of listing all the family names is to draw a picture to us that family is of great importance to God. God is trying to tell us to value our families as He values families. We are His family, all of us as the sons and daughters of Abraham. When we accept His ways, we are being accepted as children of one God (God of Abraham, Isaac, and Jacob).

As we have seen so far, there is not much written about Jabez except that we find him only in two Bible verses. The line that caught the attention of most of us and made his prayer to be one of the most powerful prayers is due to the fact that God heard his prayer and saw his tears and granted his request. Who wouldn't want to hear that God answered their prayers? I know I would love that very much. My dear fellow believers, God is still the same God even today. He still answers our devotion. As long as we are His children, He still cares for us even right here, right now.

In summary, all we have about Jabez is that we find him only in two verses of the Bible and that he was a more honorable man compared to his brothers. He implored four very powerful and maybe self-centered lines in his prayer. Moreover, his mother named him Jabez which means 'Pain' and 'sorrow'. There is nothing good that we can get out of his name. But again, through those four short sentences, this is where we find a key to unlock God's abundance and blessings. This is where we discover the secret and ways to tap into God's Kingdom door and get His attention.

CHAPTER TWO

The secret of Jabez Prayer

In chapter one, we had a chance to meet and discuss in details as to who the man named Jabez is. In chapter two, we are going to dig deeper into the prayer that he prayed and analyse how this very prayer gave him an opportunity to be written in the Bible. For most of us, we think that praying a whole day and a long prayer will definitely move God and capture His attention. But Jabez is showing us how merciful God is – in the sacred environment you can only speak to God in one sentence, and He will listen to you. In this case, Jabez spoke to God with only four short sentences.

"Oh, that you will BLESS ME INDEED.

And ENLARGE MY BORDERS.

And that your HAND MIGHT BE with me.

And you will keep me from evil so that it might not hurt me!

And God Granted His Request."

When I was just a little girl living with my grandparents, my grandfather the one and only Mr. Job Robinson Kisyombe taught me the importance of communicating with God through prayers. He demonstrated to me how to pray before we had dinner, and also he taught me a short prayer right before we went to bed. I can still remember my very simple, short prayer.

It goes like this:

"Our father who art in heaven.

Bless this food and bless who prepared it." In Jesus name Amen.

That was the full prayer that my grandfather taught me before we had a meal. Until now, I can still hear my late grandpa telling me, *good job Janet*, I can still see him being very proud of me after saying that short prayer. I felt good knowing that I made my grandfather proud. As I grew older, I became more creative. Now, I tend to rethink a lot.

I have managed to modify my prayers, add more words, make it fancier and pray longer, believing that making it longer will make my Father in heaven proud, moved, and impressed by my prayer. I thought that if I said a more elaborate prayer, God will see that I am more serious or sincere. That can be partly true and also that can easily go horribly wrong. In the presence of God, a short or a long prayer does not really matter. What matters most is who you pray to, the content of your prayer, and your sincerity deep down in your heart. In the later chapters, we will go deeper on how to do the right prayer.

Jabez's prayer includes four lines only. To justify it, let's dissect each line in details and dig deep into each line separately. We have part one to part four as a whole prayer.

Knowledge and Honor
My beloved, this is where the fun begins. I don't know about you, but I feel blessed to be born at this very time. Despite all the bad news that are happening all over the world, which we see daily on our televisions, this very moment is a blessed time to be a believer of God simply because we are in an era of abundance of facts/ information and education. Nowadays, we have the facts about the work of God literally at our fingertips. And this is a blessing indeed by itself. The internet and advanced

technology have made all these things possible. Since you are reading this book and many other materials out there, I just have to congratulate you and tell you that you are already at a different level in life; you are on a higher level and definitely not among the people who will perish because of lack of information.

Wikipedia defines knowledge *as facts, information, and skills acquired by a person through experience or education.* This practical understanding of a subject is power so don't let anyone tell you otherwise. Human beings are different from animals partly because humans are able to accrue understanding of something and are able to use that comprehension to our benefits. We are able to apply the accrued information in different skills that God has instilled in us. With the right description and by using it properly, you have already distinguished yourself from the less privileged class and putting yourself on a higher pedestal. You are already on a whole different level my friend, and that, on its own, is one big step ahead.

Honorable

The key point as to why I had to touch base about knowledge is to paint a picture of our book's main character, Jabez. The Bible says that Jabez was honorable among his brothers. It does not tell us why he was said to be more honorable. But one of the reasons why I think he was said to be of such great eminence, is because he was a man of great personality. As a result he was distinguished, more righteous than his brothers mainly because of his fear and true love for God. Jabez was more ethical because he had the awareness and had the know-how that God is the only one who can really alleviate all the burdens that had been hurting him for so long. It is very clear to me that Jabez had a good understanding of who God was.

If you come to think of it, this is very true even today. Look at all the people around you who live and walk in the presence of God – you will notice there is something very special and unique about them. In all God's believers, there is something honorable in them that makes you respect or look at them differently. For instance, people like Joyce Meyer, Joe Osteen, my beloved Bishop Dr. Alex Malasusa, or even your own pastor; have you ever wondered about what makes them so special? They are all human beings just like you and me, and yet there is something very distinguished about them, though, that I can't put my finger on. What is it that makes all of us look at them with great admiration or high regard? The answer is in the work of the Lord, God has found favor in them. You can all agree with me that in God's work, there is honor, respect, and sense of pure admiration. This goes to prove to you that the believers of God are more favored and are more dignified among their community members. God puts something extra special in all His anointed believers. Hence, Jabez was more honorable than his brothers simply because of his love for God, and because of that, he found favor with God.

PART ONE: OH THAT YOU WILL BLESS ME INDEED.

And ENLARGE MY BORDERS.

It is within our Godly rights to walk in a blessed life. It will be foolish of us to refuse this kind of favor. Jabez is up my alley. He cried to the God of Israel, and the first sentence that came out of his mouth was, "Father God, I pray that you would BLESS me indeed and Enlarge my Borders." 'Indeed' in this sentence means a whole lot. We wonder - Was he selfish to cry for his own blessings? Is it even right to pray such kind of prayer to God? Is it within my right that God will even agree to bless me and only me? For most of us, we are not taught to pray this kind of prayer. This kind of a prayer sounds ungodly, rude, ungrateful, selfish, and just self-centered.

Jabez here has opened our eyes and has given us a different format of praying from how most of us have been taught to pray. And I have to say that he has given us a whole lot of confidence to go to God for ourselves and our own selfish needs. Jabez is telling us that it is very much okay to pray for just me, myself and I. Simply because there is no selfish, small or big need to God. How I know this to be true – it is very simple and the answer is in one word, 'Bible'.

True Word

Jabez's prayer is written in the Bible for a very good reason and a good purpose. For us Christians, we believe all that is written in the good book of God to be true. The one true word we call Bible. That Word is there for a purpose, the Word is there to teach us something, and sharpen our ways of walking with the Lord. Same goes to this prayer; it has found its way in the Bible to give us a strong message about a self-centered kind of prayer. Hence, we can go to God with an attitude of boldness. Our God is a merciful God. He tells us, 'My children, it is all right to come to Me for your own personal selfish needs.' It is okay to go to God and pray for more. That is not being greedy, but it gives us a sense of knowing and coming to the realization that we are saved by a God of more than enough, the abundant God, the creator of heaven and earth.

Abundant Blessings.

On John 14:2; Jesus gives us a glimpse of heaven where God resides. He promised us that

"In my Father's house are many mansions:
If it were not so, I would have told you. I go to prepare a place for you."

In a very simple English language and in our humanly kind of thinking, the word Mansion *means large and impressive house.* In our lives here today, whoever owns a mansion is believed to be a well off individual. Without going deeper and thinking much of what Jesus was telling us, He said that in heaven there is not just one mansion, but many, abundant mansions… This is simply telling us that the God we serve is not a mediocre God. In a simple language, God is abundantly and exceedingly rich beyond compare. He is God of more than enough. He is the creator of heaven and earth. So it is within our very right to go to Him and beg for more. What we think is more to us, believe me, is nothing compared to what God owns. Jabez was very right to go to God and say, *Father, please bless me indeed –bless me abundantly. Give me more than what I have now. Give me more than what You had already given me.*

God of More than enough Love

1 John 4:9 says - This is how God showed His love among us: He sent His one and only begotten Son into the world that we might live through Him. When we accept Jesus as the son of God, we are accepting God as our father. As His children, we are entitled to His abundant blessings. It is up to us to accept His love and favors. We are already blessed today; it is just a matter of accepting the gift that is our birthright. Since Jesus came and died for our sins, He took with Him all the sorrows and pains of our world. It is in our power to accept this gift that is already handed to us.

This love of God is already handed to us today and it is not something that we will have to wait to receive tomorrow.

When writing this book, I am really trying to focus on a softer side of God. A loving father and a-to-go to father. Our father, just like an earthly father, wants us to go to Him freely at any given time and talk to Him. Some people have painted God as this huge, mean God who just sits somewhere waiting for us to make mistakes and punish us. Like any father, He takes pride when we, his children, are doing well. Same is true that our sorrows pain Him – it pains Him to see us struggling just to provide the basic needs for our families. God has given us a choice to come to Him. One thing we have to understand is the fact that

He is not and absolutely not going to force us to go to Him. It has to be within our will to follow Him. It is our own choice to receive His abundant love and abundant blessings. What will you choose today? That is the question that you, and only you, can answer. Pause and reflect.

Enlarge my Borders (Territory)

Enlarge my territories, Father Give me more, advance my kingdom and my dominion so that I can be a bigger blessing to others. Enlarge my land not according to what I think you can afford but to what God you think is righteously entitled to me. Increase me ooh Father according to the richness of your glory. Here, Jabez was saying a 'the sky is the limit' kind of prayer. For whatever small blessings he had, Jabez was praying to God to increase it and make it bigger.

In other words, Jabez was saying that, *thank you for what you have already entrusted in me. But I am praying to You to expand my dominion. For whatever I have, I am expecting more. Bless me with more than what I have. For all that I have, I pray for an increase. Enlarge my Borders.* Borders in some other Bible versions has been stated as a territory or possession. Here, Jabez was taking limits off with God. He could have easily said this - *God thank you for the blessing of one house you have given me now. I am praying that you will give me a second house as an increase.* No, Jabez didn't want to limit God – he removed all the limitations. He simply left for God to provide his needs and enlarge his richness. *You are God of no boundaries, increase me, God.* Today, the word territories or a boundary does not necessarily mean land – this means the overall grandness of God. It means the capacity to do more in serving God. The increase in good health, increase in our finances and finding favor while at work, increase in love, happiness, joy, or increase in business deals. Just God expanding according to His will.

We often make mistakes by telling and limiting God on what and how He can bless us. We have in our minds that if we ask for small things, we are more than likely to receive it from God rather than asking for bigger and grander things. Jabez teaches us to expect the unexpected from God, and never to put Him in a Box of limitation. Jabez is simply showing us the power of dreaming big. He is demonstrating to us on how to face God with a bold mindset. We serve a God of more than enough.

PART TWO: YOUR HAND MIGHT BE UPON ME
For God's hand to be upon you is like walking with a bodyguard and feeling secured that nothing or no one can cause you any harm. You are protected in all areas of your life. Praying for God's hand to be upon you is to pray

for a full package and total protection over your life, your family, your job, your business, and all your possessions.

Jabez knew that acquiring blessings without having a proper protection is a risky business, so he prayed for blessings and more blessings. He also prayed for a total security to secure all that he had and protection of his own life. He prayed to walk with God at all times as his shield of armor. We live in a world that is insecure; hence we build houses with high walls, gated and big fences. We put security alarms in our houses and if God has put you in a 1% category of being rich, you hire bodyguards to secure all your precious possessions.

Praying for God's hand to be upon you is praying for God to find favor with you and shield you. You are a blessed man indeed if you are touched by the hand of God; a man who has found favor with God has found a good thing.

PART THREE: AND YOU WILL KEEP ME FROM EVIL SO THAT IT MIGHT NOT HURT ME!

Evil is real, evil is our number one enemy. Evil is something that is bad or harmful. The synonymous words are wicked, bad, wrong, immoral, sinful, foul, dishonorable, corrupt, vicious, and malicious. In short, evil is something that causes harmfulness in our walk with God. Evil is a pure devil in one sentence. Jesus, at some point, teaches us on how to pray when He cried to God not to lead us into temptations and deliver us from evil.

In the Bible, good has been associated with life while bad has been associated with death.

In Deuteronomy 30:15:

"See, I have set before you today life and good, death and evil."

The main purpose of this book is more of giving you a motivational message, to encourage people to choose well, choose good, and choose life. There are more rewards when you do good than when you do bad.

My whole purpose of rewriting the Jabez book is to give people a sense of abundance. Abundance does not just mean money – *abundance is a total, full package of God's grace.* The purpose is for us to be thirsty of having a full God's richness that we are entitled to have. Bad or evil on the other hand wants to steal that joyful life of prosperity from us.

Jabez is a great example of praying for safety and protection. He prayed for God to keep him away from enemies because otherwise, these evils could ruin everything in his life. It is very important for us to pray daily for our families to be protected from harm. Don't underestimate the power of evil. We cannot fight evil on our own, but we can pray to God to fight a good fight for us.

It is a sad case in life that the more you advance in life and the more you receive God's blessing, the more enemies you will create. I am not going to sugar-coat it and tell you that you will receive abundant blessing and live happily ever after and everyone around you is going to be happy with you. That will be me misinforming you. I am here to tell you this, whether you like it or not, as you advance in life, some people are not going to line up with you. There are those who are not going to enjoy that journey with you, and some will go ahead of your way and try to block you. But as a believer of God, I have good news; fear not because if God is for you, no one will be against you. And as long as you shield your life in God's armor, no weapon formed against you will ever prosper. Let God fight a good battle for you since God is equipped with a full army. Let go and let God.

Don't go your ways and start fighting with a jealous relative, or a jealous neighbor, or a jealous friend. And, honestly, most of the time, an enemy is someone who knows a great deal about you. Most of the time, it is someone who is very close to you who knows all your struggles, and they are the ones who notice that you are now favored by God and that your life is changing for the better. If you start fighting with an enemy, you won't win. You will make more mess out of what is already a big mess. Just keep on doing good things. Keep on enjoying your new found abundance of joy. Your part is to pray for your enemies and pray for your protection against them and leave the fight to be between your enemies and God.

In 2 Chronicles 20:15:

"Do not be afraid! Don't be discouraged by this mighty army, For the battle is not yours, but God's."

PART FOUR: AND GOD GRANTED JABEZ'S REQUEST

God answered Jabez's prayer. That line alone made Jabez's prayer one of the most talked about and powerful prayer to this date. Just imagine if God would have denied his request, we wouldn't have been sitting here today talking about Jabez. Jabez would have easily been an ancient history. But today, we are talking and writing about him simply because God gave Jabez the seal of approval.

In Matthew 7:7, Jesus is giving us the principal of having our prayers answered. Jesus is saying:

"Ask and it will be given to you;
Seek and you will find;
Knock and the door will be opened to you."

Everyone who asks receives; the one who seeks finds; and to the one who knocks, the door will be opened. You have to ask for a blessing for it to be given to you. If you ask for provision, yes, indeed, provision will be given to you. The Bible is telling us in a simple, short version that you have not received because you didn't ask for it. God gives us what we have actually enquired Him to bless us with. Again, I cannot emphasize this enough that God is waiting for us to go get what is righteously ours. He is waiting for us to ask Him first.

In New Living Translation, it says:

"You want what you don't have, so you scheme and kill to get it.
You are jealous of what others have, but you can't get it,
So you fight and wage war to take it away from them.
Yet you don't have what you want because you don't ask God for it."

Don't be jealous of other's abundant blessings when you yourself didn't ask God to bless you. God blesses each and every one of us in a different capacity according to what we can handle. Also, God has His own timetable – His timing is not our timing, but He is never late. Keep on believing that your time is coming. There is a right time for everything and that each and every one of us has their own time to receive their portion of blessings.

You may have asked God for an increase and prayed almost every day. If you see that your prayers have not yet been answered, be patient. Remember there is a waiting time period – a period that God is preparing us to receive what we have prayed for. Also, it is what I call a **testing period**. You have to pass a test of being obedient while waiting for your turn to reap what you have planted. A waiting period simply means **your season of harvesting hasn't passed** yet.

The one who seeks finds: *Seek is an attempt or desire to achieve something. In short, seek is more about taking action.* Work for it, toil for it, fight for it. Just do something about what you have asked God to bless you with. The Bible is telling us to ask, seek, and knock, as you have asked God to fulfill your dream. But what actions are you taking to transform your dreams into a reality? I always say that we must give God something to bless. When you ask God, you are putting God to work for you, and when God goes to work on your behalf, you'd better get up and do something as well.

As the one who knocks, the door will be opened. There is a very big significance about the door. When you knock is when you are really entering into the presences of God. When you think about knocking, you automatically think of the door – the entrance, stepping inside God's presence.

This last stage is when everything you have been asking and searching for is finally going to be revealed to you. The doors to the presence of God are closed. Hence, we are instructed to knock and the door to God's abundance will be opened to us.

Knocking represents the beginning of the revelation that is *revealed* to you. Jesus also refers to Himself as a door – *no one comes to the Father except through me.* Jesus declared in John 10:9, *"'I am the door; if anyone enters through me, he shall be saved, and shall go in and out, and find pasture."* Jesus promises us to knock and the door will be opened, and once this door is opened, no man can shut this and what God has blessed, no man can curse. Once we enter this door, more will be revealed to us. This is when the hard work pays off. Jesus is instructing us when we pray to always ask, seek, and knock.

In summary of this chapter two, I am putting Jabez to be right up there on my number one list of my best friends. He and I can hang out together and just sit down with a cup of hot tea in a cool foggy weather, sitting in front of a fire pit and have a long day chatting. Jabez was a very smart and a very wise man who found a key to unlock the door of God's kingdom. He must have sat down first and figured out what it is that he needed from God. He must have first put much thought to all that he needed from God before he presented himself in front of the Lord.

In short, the prayer of Jabez shows that he prayed for blessings, he prayed for increase, he prayed to walk with God at all times and be under God's wings. Lastly, he prayed for God to fight his battles for him. That is what's needed in our daily lives. What else can you add? For me, with all that has been listed in a Jabez's prayer, I am pretty much covered. I am satisfied and that is all I need. I am good here. Life is not all that complicated. Make your life simple, sit back, and just smell the roses.

CHAPTER THREE

Cast your fears to one true God

(As Jabez cried to God of Israel).

"God's instruction to all of us....
Fear not, for I am with you; be not dismayed, for I am
your God;
I will strengthen you, I will help you,
I will uphold you with my righteous right hand."
- Isaiah 41:10

When fear hits, when difficulties arise, or when darkness
occurs in one's life, it is in our nature to worry and it
becomes easy to think the worst. At the time of difficulties,

at a time when you feel that your world has turned against you – these are the moments when you need a guarded mind the most. You need to remain in a positive mindset and leave everything in God's care. I know what you are thinking right now, you are thinking that it is easier to say than do. You are very right. There are some moments one cannot see any light.

They say 'time heals everything,' but I am not sure if I totally agree with this statement. All I know in regards to this well-known saying is this: if you give enough time to any issue or problem you will be in a better position to think clearly and solve a problem. Also, it gives you a prime chance to turn to God and give God time to work on your matter. Any issue or problem appears to be massive when it first occur. And this can be mainly due to anxiety and panic feeling, which hinders you from thinking clearly. But as time progresses, what seemed impossible becomes a bit lighter and solvable with a clear solution.

I have worked in a psych unit in the hospital. One of the ways to calm an agitated patient is to remove them from a noisy place and send them to a quiet place, or to give a patient a walk in a garden, have fresh air, remove them from an environment that is causing an increase in their agitation. Sometimes we direct an aggravated person to go to a quite room and stay there for a while. This gives them time to cool down, and reflect on their behaviors. In this case, yes, we can say that time heals everything. God can do things that are unseen by human eyes. Go to him faithfully believing that He will give you guidance and a sense of wisdom. I do believe that in every problem there is a solution. Just give it time.

While waiting for God to heal and remove the mountains, this is the time to pray without ceasing and increase your faith that God is at work. Hence, cast your fears to one true God. It does not matter how long you are going to pray but if your sacred environment is not of the one true God, then I am sorry to say that you will be wasting your precious time. In John 14:6, Jesus said: *"I am the way and the truth and the life. No one comes to the Father except through Me. If you had known Me, you would know My Father as well."*

Before we start to pray, it is important to recognize that the prayer goes to the right place and to the right person. Imagine when you are writing a very important letter and you put a wrong address on it, no matter how much money and how fast you want your letter to reach its final destination, if you have a wrong address, you will just be wasting your money and effort and the letter will probably be returned back to the sender, or it will most likely be lost in transition.

The big lesson we are getting from Jabez's prayer is the environment that he created prior to starting his prayer. He knew exactly to whom he had to cast his fears. There are different ways you can create a sacred environment. Some invite the Holy Spirit before they start praying. Whatever you do, just have it in your mind that whenever you are saying a prayer, you are entering the holy land of God, you are knocking the doors of God and that you are confirming that you have the right address. Don't just pour your feelings to just anybody, rather pour them to God.

We only have one true God. I cannot emphasize this enough. The God who created this earth is the same God yesterday, today and tomorrow. The God of Abraham, Isaac and Jacob; 'I am who I am' is the only one true living God and is the one we need to cast our fears to.

In so many places in the Bible, it was written over and over again that one thing that really upsets God, is seeing His beloved children praying to other gods – who are not the one true God. We have seen that in the Bible where God got so mad He destroyed the whole world and everything in it. This act of worshiping other things rather than the true God really gets into God's nerves. Our Father is merciful in so many ways, but in several verses in the Bible, we have seen how angry God gets when we go to false gods for help. As a parent, I am sure you will feel bad as well if your children go to your neighbors for help or for answers, especially if you don't like that particular neighbor, and you know for sure that this neighbor cannot help your children and will possibly give poor and bad pieces of advice. I am sure you will feel angry and jealous at the same time. Now, imagine how God feels when you turn to false gods for help.

Exodus 34:14 says:

"You shall worship no other God: for the LORD, whose name is Jealous, is a jealous God."

Joshua 24:19 says:

Then Joshua said to the people,

"You will not be able to serve the LORD, for He is a holy God. He is a jealous God; He will not forgive your transgression or your sins.

We will be right if we say that Jabez didn't want to get into God's bad side. Right from the start, he understood this one simple, yet powerful secret – he gathered the right address to send his prayers. He understood there is only one God. The Bible says *Jabez cried to the Lord of Israel, the one true living God.*

In Psalm 72:18: you will notice the keyword ALONE.

"Blessed be the LORD God, the God of Israel, Who ALONE works wonders."

I am really having fun and enjoying writing about the work of the Lord. You don't have to look further to get the answers. All the answers to everything are within the Bible. On the verse above, it tells us that the Lord of Israel is the only God who alone works wonders. By definition, the word 'wonder' means <u>a feeling of surprise mingled with admiration, caused by something beautiful, unexpected, unfamiliar, or inexplicable</u>. And that is what our amazing Father can do for us. Why on earth does one look for other nonliving gods when one has a one true God who can do the inexplicable?

CHAPTER FOUR

Dare to Dream Big – Pray a Bold Prayer

Proverbs 23:7

For as he thinks in his heart, so is he.
"Eat and drink!" he says to you,
but his heart is not with you

The Prayer of Jabez is all about being bold while presenting yourself in front of the Lord. It is about coming into full realization of who you really are; you are a child of the most high God and there is nothing mediocre about you. Have you ever reached a point in your life where you feel totally fed up with all that is going on in your life? A point where you say to yourself, "Enough is enough. I am done, and something must change." At this exact point in your life, we find our friend, Jabez. When Jabez kneeled to God, it looks more like he really needed things to change. He came to a realization that it is possible to get more out of his current life. In short, his devotion is about believing in impossibilities. It is a solemn request for help and having a strong faith in the heavenly Father.

Sometimes failure and difficulties of lives are your best friends. Most inventions were discovered because of the need or difficulties that arose. For whatever it is that you are going through today, you are reminded not to face it all alone. There is a redeemer who is anxiously waiting to hear from you. Jesus died on a cross for this one purpose, to take the heavy weight off our backs. Never ask yourself and doubt yourself by saying, *"Is it really possible for me to reach my dreams?"* Neither should you start asking yourself how you are going to get there. Remove all the doubts of 'how.' Don't put limits on God's abilities. His ways are not our ways. He is our creator and He knows how you are going to reach there. While you are contemplating, don't let your current situation define who you are tomorrow. Don't make the mistake of letting your current situation tell what you can be and what you cannot do. Conjure up big and just rely on God. He is the ruler of the universe and our only source of all moral authority, the supreme being of limitless.

My own mother, Dr. Victoria Kisyombe, is my main inspiration and my living proof that God exists today. She lost her husband at a very young age of 36 years old. At this point, she was left with three young children to take care. My brother Daniel didn't know any better at this point and my sister, Dr. Nai, was just a baby of less than one year old. She was just in diapers when our father died suddenly. For anyone, it is always hard to lose a spouse. There are so many things that'll change after a big loss like that. For most African families, especially for us, we were immediately affected economically. Overnight, our family went from having two earnings to just depending on mom's small income alone. Our small family had to relocate from a house we were all accustomed, moving to a totally new big city. Everything from that point on changed completely, and we were all forced to adapt to this new uncertain life.

In any household, especially in the African economy, where there is nothing like life insurance or any kind of spousal support after death, many families can really feel the impact of losing a beloved one. For us, Life was tough and rough, but that didn't stop my mother. She struggled all alone, and through all this, she managed to make us feel complete. For all the challenges and hardness of life she faced, I give credit to her for her impressive drive and courage. She had to persevere and push herself to become the woman I see today. I always say it took the death of my father to awaken a very shy, humble woman to a one fantastic, fearless, motivational woman whose sky is only the limit.

In Dr. Victoria's life biography, there is nothing too small or too difficult for her. She has received so many awards for her impressive work. The most memorable prestige award was the one she received in the year 2014. Because of my mother's unyielding commitment to economic empowerment of women in Tanzania, she was awarded by Hillary Clinton through Vital Voices Global Partnership, which she is a founder. – "Annual Global Leadership in Economic Empowerment Award". Vital Voices said that my mother's vision and innovative spirit her apart as a global role model and that the significance of her work will be felt for generations to come. Through her path of success and pushing boundaries in doing what she does best, and that is micro-leasing, motivating and inspiring women all over the world, my mother has always gracefully walked this path with God. Despite her multiple travels all over the world in her journey to go inspire other women, Dr. Victoria has always remained humble. I have learned so much by just watching her life journey. She is a big dreamer, a go-getter, and once she sets up her mind to achieve a particular goal, she makes sure that goal becomes a reality. Multiple failures in life never stop her from pursuing the impossibilities. As of today, my mother's profile has reached a staggering number of 27,000 women and counting. These are the women that in one way or another have financially benefited from a simple, humble woman who dared to dream big. She has lived her life through Deuteronomy 31:6, which says: "Be strong and courageous. Do not be afraid or terrified because of them, for the LORD your God goes with you; he will never leave you nor forsake you."

There are so many dreams, whether small and big. If you categorize yourself in a small portion dream, I guarantee that even your end results will be small, but if you take limits off God and stretch your faith and ruminate big dreams, your end results will absolutely reflect that you're thinking big. Biblically, we are reminded again by Proverbs 23:7 that for as he thinks in his heart, so is he. This simply means that if you consider yourself as someone who deserves less, you will definitely get less. There is no harm in upgrading your value in your very own mind. Hence, the topic of big imagination. For example, if you live in a compacted one-bedroom rented apartment today, why not dare to muse yourself that you are living in a five bedroom, two-story house that is fully owned by you? Or if you are in a house paying monthly mortgage today, I challenge you to start contemplating and seeing yourself living a mortgage-free house in five years tops.

Same goes with visualization. Start visualizing yourself doubling your income in the next one year. In five years' time, your income will be ten times more than what you are currently earning. If you are a business owner, visualize that your business is growing and expanding. Engrave in your unconscious mind that particular thing that you want to own. Visualize it; dream it, just live within your la-la land. Think this way: what do you have to lose by dreaming and thinking big?

For you to reach your final destination, where you really want to be, you must have a clear roadmap. You have to conceptualize where you want to be at a certain time frame. Have a clear picture and channel it to what your naked eyes cannot see – and this is what we call *dreaming*. You have to see yourself being comfortable in your final destination even before you get there. Dare to think and dream big and never ask how you are going to get there. For any aspiration to come true, you have to visualize it first. To make your dream a reality, you have to see it first as a reality, live in it and just believe and have total faith that it will come to past. If your goal is to move from point A to point B; start seeing yourself at point B, live at point B, and make yourself comfortable at point B. Fantasize about it. Dream and paint a picture in your mind that you are already getting settled at point B.

In summary, there are three very simple steps that you will have to take to make your dream a reality.

⇨ First thing first, start with a dream, visualize, paint a clear picture of the exact thing that you want to accomplish, and see yourself within the final destination, which is perceived by you to be wonderful or perfect.

⇨ Second, pray about it then ask God to give you ways on how you are going to reach your goals. Be diligent about whatever you are going to do, but always be grateful of your current situation now.

⇨ Third, work hard where you are planted. Just do something about it, take action, and act upon your plan - don't dream and go to sleep expecting that your objectives will come to pass and come true.

Remember again and again that God is a rewarder of working hands.

By doing those three steps above, eventually, God will grant your wishes. You will be surprised how quick and soon your intentions are going to be fulfilled. We serve a God of more than enough, an abundant God, and the God of the universe. Whatever you think may be too big to you is very small compared to the richness of our Father.

There is nothing more important in life than investing in yourself. Be of understanding that Education and familiarity gained by experience of a fact is a key to making big in anything in this life – study, learn, spend time in the library, know and believe that cognizance is power and not just a myth. Always strive to do something to make yourself better. Develop a tendency to read. If you want to do investment business, why not start finding materials about investment, financing, self-development, money/business management and just educate yourself.

On your search of answering a question as to how you will make your dream come true – It is also a good idea to pray to God to give you wisdom, knowledge, and understanding. We see that in Daniel 1:17, the four young men were given knowledge, intelligence, and wisdom and as for Daniel, he was even given the power to understand visions and dreams.

In the matter of helping your dreams come true, you are also advised to share your intent with someone. Speak it out. There is something that will unlock within you when you speak out. Achievements tend to become more believable when you speak out the words. Hence, there is power in the words of our tongues.

Also, in the matter of sharing, be careful not to share your plans with someone who is short-minded. Share your vision with someone you know can believe in you. Someone who can support you and give you the encouragement and constructive feedback you need. Be watchful; share a big vision with a person who is also a monumental thinker. And if your end results are very powerful, and you feel like no one in your circle of friends can even understand it, then start looking outside your circle. Be mindful of the fact that some achievements and blessings are best to be kept private within a small like minded group of people.

Bible teachings are telling us to love one another. This is very true and is a principal element that we need to follow. Although in the mind of love, don't be mistaken with the fact that in life you will always have two groups of people: One group will be for you, cheer you up every step of the way. The other side is the group I call heavy baggage or weeds; they always add unnecessary weight and just slow you down. If you are not careful, they will cloud your judgement, vision, and your way of thinking. No matter how much you like them, they will not walk with you in your journey of success. And these groups of people, unfortunately, can be just about anyone, mostly the person who is close to you. Be careful in choosing who to associate with. You cannot choose your family members, but you can definitely choose and select an associate/friend.

We don't get to choose our families, but families choose us. Never make the mistake of being ashamed of your descendants no matter how horrible they seem. Appreciate their presence whether they are for you or not, they are still part of you. First and foremost, they are the reasons we are who we are today. But that does not mean that conflict does not occur among bloodline members. I had to include descents here because this is another group that tends to know you very well. They also have already categorized you in a box where they think you fit in best. Normally, this group will be the hardest group to believe in your vision and dreams. If you are lucky, you will have two or three people who can support you in your journey and your crazy ideas. If this is the case in your life just know that you are not alone and this is very typical to many people. Sometimes, families, in the name of love and providing protection for you, will cause you not to pursue your dreams. They will stop you from taking risks. As a result, it is very healthy if you believe in yourself first, don't wait for people to tell you what you can and cannot do.

We love our lineage and we love our friends, but at the same time, without bad intentions, our loved ones can create a too safe and comfortable environment for us. Sometimes safe, risk-free, comfortable and casual environment does not challenge us to grow. I am very thankful to my mother to have given me a chance to leave her pleasant nest just immediately after I left high school. I left home at a very young age and came to America. While living far away from home was a very challenging, rough and tough life. On the other hand, I now know that, this same path was inevitable for my today's destination. The roughness and tough challenges of living all alone have created the woman I am today. Looking back, I wish I could have changed so many mistakes that I have done in the past. I understand that all what happened, my life experiences, was a very necessary growth process to go through. For all my past poor judgment caused by poor reasoning or simply carelessness, I do understand now all that was in my good old days. I can't keep on reliving my past. In short, what was tough, rough, and just plainly painful made me strong and courageous at this very moment. Just learn from your mistakes and difficulties, and move to the next day.

Make a habit of surrounding yourself with people who can inspire you, who can challenge you to move forward, and who can share good information with you. In short, hang out and fly with eagles. For eagles, there is practically no limit, they tend to fly very high with ease. They always strive for the best with little or no fear. Eagles will inspire you to soar to places of unknown. To the indefinite extent where you never dreamed of going.

CHAPTER FIVE

Praying with Faith and Obedience

Since this book is all about prayer, I have found out that it is important we talk about faith and obedience. We say a prayer in confidence and believing that our God is listening to us. A prayer without conviction is the same as a Swahili proverb, "Kutwanga maji kwenye kinu." This is the same as doing a hard job without fruitful results. You will just be wasting your time and energy. We have been instructed to pray with great trust until we receive it. Faith simply believes in the unknown. The Bible tells us that faith is the confidence that what we hope for will actually happen; it gives us an assurance about things we cannot see. You actually say a prayer and hope that it will happen according to His will. For God is instructing us to have total confidence in Him and total belief that He is a living God. When it comes to the matter of total trust, God is not asking much of you, all He wants is for you to have as little faith as a mustard seed. Even that is enough to make mountains move.

Hebrew 11:6 says that:

"And without faith it is impossible to please Him,
For he who comes to God must believe
That He is a rewarder of those who seek Him."

I would like you to note something here −the Keyword "Impossible". We all know that there is nothing impossible to God, but yet here, the same Bible is telling us that without faith, it is impossible to please God. Now you can see how powerful faith is. Faith is as vital to the Christian believers as it is oxygen vital to our daily living. All living creatures require air to survive and have life. Similarly, every prayer needs faith to please God. Matthew 21:21-22 - And Jesus answered and said to them, "Truly I say to you, if you have faith and do not doubt, you will not only do what was done to the fig tree, but even if you say to this mountain, 'Be taken up and cast into the sea,' it will happen. And all things you ask in prayer, believing, you will receive."

An Act of Obedience

As having a total conviction is vital to a prayer, the same is said about obedience. *Obedience is an act or practice of obeying; compliance with an order, request, or an act of being submissive to another's authority.* In short, the word obedience signifies "to hear," or "to listen". How can we serve God when our hearts are not obliging to His word? Jesus as the son of God is a master of obedience to His Father. It is a known fact that Jesus was compliant even to the time of His death. It is also true that an amenable child finds favor in the Lord.

Proverbs 3:4:

"My children find favor, good understanding,
And high esteem in the sight of the Lord, and in the sight of man."

It is a very good thing to find favor in God. God as a living God has a purpose and plan for all of us as His children. To find favor with the Lord is to find a total, full package of life's abundance.

We all know the story of Joseph, son of Jacob. It has been said that he is the one who enjoyed Almighty's favor among all his brothers. Joseph, the son of Jacob, found favor with God; literally, overnight, he went from being a prisoner to becoming the second- in- chief next to the Pharaoh. Today, on the book shelves, we see many books of people's stories about their journey from poverty to prosperity. Joseph is the originator and a true definition of "From rags to riches" story. This is when a person rises from poverty to wealth, and in some cases, from absolutely nothing to the heights of extreme abundance. And for Joseph, it happened overnight simply because he found favor with the Highest. He found favor with heavenly father because he was obedient to God. Joseph is also said to have been more honorable than his brothers. His brothers meant for evil, but God meant for good. His brothers sold him into slavery, but little did they know that they were sending him to a land of blessings.

Even during the tough times, Joseph refused to give up hope; he refused to give up his faith in God. He remained obedient to God despite all the difficulties that he was facing. If you read in depth about the story of Joseph you will easily find out that Joseph was submissive to his father Jacob and that he strongly had a fear of God. God was moved by his obedience, and as a result, Joseph was blessed beyond his wildest dreams.

How can I be a blessing to others when my own life is not blessed?

Has this ever happened to you: when someone in need comes to you asking for your very last dollar that you have in your pocket? How can I be a blessing to others when my own life is not blessed? This question reminds me a great deal of the widow at Zarephath (Commonly known as the story of Elijah and a widow with a jar of flour and a jug of oil). The story was about a hungry Elijah who commanded a poor widow to go and bring him a morsel (a small piece) of bread and water in a vessel so that he could drink. After hearing this, I can picture a woman looking at Elijah like, you must be joking right now. How can I be of service to you when what I have is not even enough for me and my son? As you can see, she went on saying this: "I am gathering few fire sticks so that we can eat our last meal and wait to die." You talk about hitting a rock bottom. Her pantry of food was so empty to a point that this widow found peace with death.

And now, God is coming with the biggest temptation of all. *Give me all that is left.* How can I be a blessing to you when I don't even feel blessed myself? In the end, the widow obeyed and went to do as Elijah requested. God is indeed a rewarder of all rewarders. The Bible tells us that the widow and her son were greatly blessed with abundance and had plenty to eat simply because of the act of a widow's obedience. She obeyed the voice of God to go and give all that she had left. As a result, God blessed her beyond measure. The widow and her son didn't die of starvation. The story continues on to say that through her act of obedience, her jar of flour and her jug of oil never ran dry for many days until the dry season was over.

Different Ways to Pray

They are so many ways to communicate with God. If we explore all the ways in saying a prayer, I believe we will need another whole book just to talk about the different styles of saying a prayer. But since we are on a topic of prayers, we will just mention a few and look into them.

The picture I want you to understand here is that there are many ways to pray to God. All ways and all kind of praying styles are welcomed. Who can say that there is only one way and the best way to communicate with God? Nobody.

Prayers can be rich and very powerful when they are meaningfully straight to the point and just short. Also, prayers can be long, requiring more effort which may take several days or weeks. Some people pray and fast as well. We see both of these styles in the Bible. One is when Esther who prayed while fasting for three days before she went to meet her husband, the king. In addition, we see Jabez's prayer, which is short and simple right to the core. In both of these situations, the prayers were answered. Whether it is a long or short prayer, as long as it is within the sacred moment, God will answer your request.

You can decide to hold a prayer in a group of believers and non-believers, or just pray with one of your friends. I personally have used a number of tactics of saying a prayer. At times, the spirit of God moves you to pray with your pastor/priest/preacher because you feel the need to partner with the servants of God to put more meaning to your prayer. In fact, it has been written in Matthew 18:20, *"for where two or three gather in my name, there am I with them."* Whichever way you choose to communicate with God is fine. We have been advised to pray without ceasing.

Matthew 6: 9–13 – "The Lord's Prayer"

Since I am in a chapter of talking about prayer, I am obliged to talk about another very powerful prayer that Jesus Himself left for us to use. This is the prayer that was shown to us by Jesus Christ. Commonly known as "The Lord's Prayer". Some simply calls it "Our Father or Pater

Noster" among other names. Through reading about the son of God, it is impossible for one not to notice that Jesus saying a prayer to God was truly vital. Through His ways of living, Jesus has demonstrated over and over again the importance of speaking with God through prayer.

One of his disciples asked Jesus to teach them to pray and Jesus didn't hesitate to do so. But before Jesus taught His disciples on how to pray, he laid down some ground rules. We see that Jesus warned all of us that when praying, do not heap up empty words (in other words, do not repeat the same words over and over again like a parrot)... Jesus said the Gentiles *"pour out a flood of empty words"* because they think they will be heard for saying many words; don't pray like this. Jesus was instructing all of us to be careful, not just to recite words without even putting a meaning to the words we are praying for.

When praying to God, be sincere about what you are praying about. Be aware of your words, and what you are telling God. The prayer should be meaningful. Just refrain from the habit of reciting a prayer aimlessly without a purpose and hoping that your prayer will be answered by God. In short, Jesus was telling us to be mindful of when we are talking with God.

Hence, Jesus showed us how to pray. He said, "Pray like this:

Our Father who is in heaven,

Hallowed be your name.

Your kingdom come,

Your will be done, on earth as it is in heaven.

Give us this day our daily bread,

And forgive us our debts,

As we also have forgiven our debtors.

And lead us not into temptation, but deliver us from evil.

For yours is the kingdom and the power and the Glory forever Amen."

I wouldn't have done justice to my book if I didn't include the prayer above. In a way, I see the resemblance and similarities between the prayer of Jesus and the prayer of Jabez. Except that Jabez used this phrase "me and I" in his prayer, while Jesus used the phrase *us* throughout His prayer. E.g. Give us, deliver us, and forgive us.

⇨ The strong similarities that jump out at me are the fact that Jesus and Jabez both created holy ground at the beginning of a prayer by casting their prayer to God. In Jesus' prayer, He started by saying, "Our Father who art in heaven," while the prayer of Jabez started by saying, "Jabez cried to the God of Israel." By calling upon the name of the Lord; you are declaring that you are about to enter the holy ground of God. There is no room for the devil at that point as your mind is very clear as to whom you want to talk to. At this point, the only person you want to talk to is God, and you are able to do that by calling His name. By doing so, you are writing the right address on your prayer envelope and confirming that your prayer is directed straight to one living God.

⇨ Second similarity is the fact that they all prayed for the blessing from God. Jesus said, "Give us this day our daily bread." *'Bread'* in this case represents favor and blessing from God. Bread is used *as something that fulfils our lives*. Also, note that Jesus used the word 'today' as in present tense and not tomorrow. He didn't say Father bless us whenever or bless us tomorrow. He was very specific by asking for the blessings to be given today. While Jabez on his prayer, he was more direct by saying *bless me indeed*. The word *Bless* in this context is the same as Bread in Jesus' prayer. And note that when Jabez said *Bless me*, he also prayed in a present tense. As in a current language, this confirms to us that the miracles of God are of now and God is always in a present mode.

⇨ The third similarity I have found is how they both prayed to God to keep us and shield us from evil so that it does not cause any harms in our lives. As evil is the number one enemy that destroys our relationship with God, Jesus and Jabez both declared to us that evil is real, and it is not something that we should take lightly as it can destroy us. The good news is that we should not be frightened as we pray for God's hand to be upon us and protect us at all times. We are instructed to pray without ceasing for God's protection over our lives and our beloved ones and everything that surrounds us.

⇨ The fourth similarity that I see is the fact that Jesus and Jabez didn't wait for us to be in heaven to start enjoying and experiencing God's blessings. They both called for heaven to come down here on earth today. Jesus, in his prayer, said, "Your kingdom come, Your will be done, on earth as it is in heaven." He graciously prayed for God's kingdom to be here on earth today. Same as Jabez prayer as he prayed to start receiving his increase in abundant blessings today while here on earth rather than waiting to experience it while he is in heaven. We are being taught that we can start having heavenly experiences today here on planet on which we live.

CHAPTER SIX

The Spirit of Giving and Blessings

I seriously should have put this chapter on my introduction page – on the very first page of the book. I am saying that because the act of giving, has always been the one of the main key ingredients to unlock the provision of God's supernatural blessings. Giving and blessings are like twins – they are right there on the same line. You should call yourself blessed if you have no issues in the department of giving. But be careful as not to confuse the spirit of giving and helping others together with tithing. In this chapter, we will discuss all these two traits in detail. They are quite similar but different in a way, and they both hold the key to the abundance of the door of God's blessings.

The last message from my Grandmother

I have already shared with you that I was raised mostly by my late grandparents. For some people, when you tell them that you are a product of your grandparents, they start feeling sorry for you. They should not be sorry because that was the best thing that has ever happened in my life. I wouldn't change it for anything. My childhood memories with my grandparents are the best, full of love, and I have to say I am not a troubled person today simply because of how I was nurtured.

One Monday afternoon, I was sitting in the very front pew in the church, and this was a very sad day because I was sitting in a church service for my grandmother's funeral, Mrs. Elise Kisyombe. I had already done some counseling in my head that I know she's gone. It was a sad day, but I had to be strong for my family. I had to be there for my grandmother. I was determined that I would be there for my grandmother until the very last minute we put her in the ground. So, I had to take control of my emotions and tears. I had to make sure that everything in my grandmother's funeral was going right. Why? Because my grandmother and my grandfather have always been there for me. So, on her funeral day, I just had to be strong like how I knew she needed me to be. And this was my way of telling her *thank you for being the best grandmother ever*. This was my way of telling her that I was there with her, and there for her, even at the time of her funeral.

My grandparents have always been my cheerleaders and my life coaches. The church was packed with people. I have to add that this is the same church that I grew up attending when I was a young girl living with my grandparents. Back inside the Forest Moravian Church in Mbeya, Tanzania, it brought me back to many childhood memories. At this time, there were so many nice things spoken about my grandmother there at the church. Now it was time for a group of church women to give their speech or farewell message to my grandmother. My grandmother was a member of this group – they call it *"kitulano"*. Kitulano in simple English means *'being there for one another.'* One member came in front of the church, she didn't even have her speech written up, and she started praising my grandmother on her character of being a great giver. My grandmother had been sick for a long time, but all this time, each and every month, she would send her small portion of money to the church as her tenth percent, and also she would send her contribution to this particular women's group.

This woman started praising my grandmother that even on that day when my grandma was lying cold in her coffin; the group had just received the money from her, of which she did send to them before she was called to be with the Lord. That means even in her very last breath, her mind was in the Lord. And that was not all of it. I was not shocked since I knew about her habit of giving to God every month. It was not a secret. She was generous and fond of giving. But what moved me the most on that day is the fact that this lady, while giving her speech, pointed out that the very location of the church we were praising God in (the land where the church was built) was once donated to the church by my grandparents. I had chills to hear that. What a great testimony to hear. Something in my body just stood still. How come no one ever told me about this before? I asked myself how this woman can remember this and I didn't. Then, I turned to my grandma as if I wanted her to say something about this. I looked at her face; she was just lying there quietly looking more glorious than ever and very peaceful. All I could say to her was *thank you*. Little did I know that even to her very last day, my grandmother had a very strong advice to give me. I know it was not just me in the church that day, but I felt like I was all alone with her and she was giving me this great message.

It felt like she was telling me: *"Janet - you have to develop a spirit of giving. You have to be somebody and when you leave this world, you leave behind love, a fascinating story and a great legacy."* The message was very clear in my mind. I felt like that was a message just for me, and it is something my grandma wanted to tell and leave behind for me. I closed my eyes and thanked God for my grandparents' lives. I prayed to God to instill in me the same spirit of giving that He instilled in them. Surely, what you give in secret, God will reward you in the open. My grandparents were rewarded by God in the open in front of a big mass full of friends and family members.

What is a Spirit of Giving?

Having a spirit of giving is the same as having a heart of provision. A person with a heart of provision is indeed blessed. There are so many forms of giving. Giving can be offerings in church, and also giving does not necessarily have to be in monetary terms. The spirit of giving can be in any form of assistance, e.g. helping an old lady crossing a road safely, helping your sick neighbor mow the lawn, visiting the sick in the hospital, being a good friend to your friend/friends, being a shoulder to lean on for someone else, going out and having fun with your family, providing for your family's daily needs, and just being a good role model to everyone else.

Being a person with the spirit of giving means doing good, which is not necessarily for you, but for someone else. A person with a spirit of giving tends to love big. They are people with big hearts for others. God rewards people with a good character. And these are the people who bring change to the world. If you want to move the world and make a difference, just start small, start with your own surroundings and everything that surrounds you. Anyone can make a change and have a big impact in the world.

10th percent.

The spirit of giving and blessings are all wrapped-up in one sentence for very good reasons. You are a very blessed man or woman if giving comes to you naturally. A prayer without giving is nothing. Same goes to tithing. My friend, since you are reading this book, I believe we all want the same thing. We want God to bless us indeed abundantly over and above what our imaginative minds can think. But again, God can only do that if you follow His principles. If you are one of the people who think that tithing is just making a pastor rich, or just wasting your time and money, my friend I will say *'think again.'* You are probably missing out a lot on God's daily blessings.

All those possessions you have including your cars, house, jobs, family and good health are properties of God. God wants you to send to Him what is His – what belongs to Him. Come to think of it; what actually belong to Him is not that big compared to the reward God gives us – out of 100% of what you are receiving, God wants you to return to Him only tenth percent and you keep the 90%.

Tithing is the act of giving God what is righteously His. There are so many questions involving the act of tithing. Some are arguing that tithing is the thing of the past – it is the practice of Old Testament. And that tithing was under the law not under grace (Jesus is grace). But Jesus said *He came to fulfil the law and not to abolish it* (Matthew 5:17). What I have come to learn about the Bible is that to every question we hold, there are answers written inside it. You don't have to look very far for answers. The Bible also gives us a much solid proof as to why we have to give to God what originally belongs to Him.

There are so many verses in the Bible about the topic of giving 10th percent. But I will list only two verses for now. In fact, I love this verse in Malachi 3: 10-12 so much. You will see this verse in another place in my book where God is telling us exactly the way it is. He is asking us to test Him and wait and see what happens next. In fact, in this verse,

God is boldly telling us that once you do this, you diligently give what belongs to Him. God will see your effort and bless you to the extent that all nations will call you blessed. That is a very powerful statement. God is saying *test me.* The word *test* means an *act intended to establish the quality, performance, or reliability of something.* God shows us that He is confident in what He talks about. If you tithe, you will receive your generous reward, it is as simple as that.

I beg you to start tithing today. Why not just do this to test God without hesitations?

Malachi 3:10-12
"Bring the full tithe into the storehouse, that there may be food in my house.
And thereby put me to the test," says the Lord of hosts,
"if I will not open the windows of heaven for you
And pour down for you a blessing until there is no more need.
I will rebuke the devourer for you, so that it will not destroy the fruits of your soil,
And your vine in the field shall not fail to bear," says the Lord of hosts.
"Then all nations will call you blessed, for you will be a land of delight," says the Lord of hosts.

Proverb 3:9-10 says:
Honor the LORD with your wealth, with the first fruit of
all your crops;
Then your barns will be filled to <u>overflowing</u>,
And your vats will brim with new wine.

On *Proverb 3:9-10, note* the key words "First Fruit of all".…..
And then He goes on to tell us that after you do that, you
will be filled with overflowing blessings. Overflowing
means *more than enough, it means full of abundance, over
and above.* But what comes first before you receive this
overflowing blessing is your act of obedience to give God
what is rightfully His. Both verses above are speaking a
similar language, saying tests me then I will bless you.
Give first then you will receive God's blessings.

One thing I have noticed once you develop a habit of tithing
at the church as God instructed us to do is that you start to
feel good about yourself. You get immediate gratification.
There is something in your own body that starts to shift.
This shift is a good shift, my friend. You start feeling good,
way before you start receiving God's blessings. If you have
not started giving God's tenth percent of your income, I
encourage you to start today. You are never too late. Our
God is a gracious God. He is slow to anger and quick to

forgive. He is not going to come and punish you as to why you have not been doing so all these years.

Change your life for the better. Develop a good habit. It is our choice to change and turn our lives around. It is you holding a pen and paper to write your true story – and you better do justice by writing a good story about yourself. Write a good story about your life, a life full of fulfillment, and not a mediocre life full of fear, emptiness, and uncertainty. Write a good story for many generations to come. For that change to take place, you have to start today.

Let us pray.

Father God, we thank You today and come to You with humble, obedient hearts. We call ourselves blessed today because You have instilled in us a spirit of giving and taught us to return what is righteously Yours. We thank You for the overflowing blessings that we are receiving today, and that we receive it with open arms. Father, we choose today to test You, put your word in experiment purposely knowing that Your word is the truth. In Jesus Name we praise Your Holy name. Amen.

CHAPTERS SEVEN

Ways you may be blocking your blessings

The Bible is telling us that Blessing is our birth right and it is already given to us. So if we already own the blessings, what is it that is causing us not to live the blessed life that we are entitled to? What is it that is blocking us from enjoying God's full favor? Have you ever wondered why you are working so hard every day without catching any break? You are really trying everything possible, living right, doing everything by the book, yet things continue to be hard, and while other people sail easy in life. Next, we will see some of those things that can put a block for us to enjoy God's abundance and love.

You are your own enemy

The number one factor that may be blocking your blessings today is you. You and only you is the number one enemy of your own path to receiving what is waiting for you. If you are like me, I tend to criticize myself a lot more than others criticize me. I am my own main critic. I don't need anybody else to criticize me. I do that very well on my own. I have struggled so much in this arena of seeing myself as a failure and the fact that I don't measure up. As human beings, we sometimes tend to see that other people qualify to be in higher rankings in life and not us. It is easy to picture others as more successful and make a justification for them, saying, *'oh, yes, they deserve it, they deserve to have more, they are what they are and we don't measure up to them.'* If you are like me, I will say let us stop here. We are all sons and daughters of the highest mighty God. We are all digging from the same pond of God's grace.

The Bible is teaching us not to be envious of others success but again, don't put yourself so low, to a point of blocking your own abundance. In short, we call this lack of self-confidence. It is fear of limitation that is within us, and I pray to God that this fear should be removed in Jesus name. Develop a spirit of believing in yourself, believing that you are whole and that you are more than enough in God's eyes.

Philippians 4:13(NKJV)
"I can do all things through Christ who strengthens me"

Four years ago, God gave me the vision to write this book. I kept postponing it in fear and doubt; like *who am I to write a book about Prayer? I am just Janet, not even a pastor. I am not a preacher, and I don't own a church or anything close to the church. Who do I think I am? Am I TD Jakes?* I almost blocked my own vision just because I didn't see myself fitting in. I saw myself as a small fish in a big pond. The flow of my path changed when I came to a realization that when it comes to God's work, God will use just anybody, and absolutely anybody to spread His work. And why not me? By realizing who I was and who I serve, and also realizing that I am a daughter of the higher Almighty God, God of nothing is impossible, I knew I could write this book. Hence, today, you are reading this book with me. This book almost never happened simply because I didn't think I was qualified; I didn't see myself as good enough.

God gives us visions and dreams for a reason because He knows that we are capable of doing His work and we are equally qualified to do justice to His work. I strongly believe that dreams and visions come from Higher up. It is up to us to act upon the dream and make it a reality.

While on a topic of you being the main enemy to your own development, the other part that I feel is imperative that we touch is the very fact of "holding on to the past". This is a big problem for so many people as we tend to relive the past and replay those awful experiences over and over again like a broken record. As a human being, at one point in life, you will make mistakes, some mistakes are public knowledge, and those are the ones that cost us a lot because they hurt deeply. For most celebrities, their mistakes make breaking news. The world can be very harsh. If one is not careful, as we have seen in various cases, one can end up falling into the temptations of being intoxicated just because they cannot bare the pain and agony of shame. When the past experiences become everybody's talk, for some it becomes very hard to handle. They end up hurting themselves more or even ending their own lives. Celebrities are just as human as us.

You will not be doing yourself a favor by not forgetting and forgiving yourself of the past blunders that you have done. I will advise you to be kind to yourself as Jesus is kind to us. In Psalm 103:12, the Bible is telling us that "as far as the east is from the west, so far has he removed our transgressions from us." Our Father in heaven has already forgiven us of our sins and he does not remember anymore, so why not you. It is always easier said than done, but you can try to forgive yourself and leave the past to be buried in the past. At times, you will find some friends/colleague who are still stuck in your past life, and they tend to define you by your past experiences. They always want you to remember your pain of the past. What do you do in cases like these? In cases like this, don't give an enemy power to destroy your joy and effort to move on in life. What I have learned is that you cannot change what people think of you, but you can change what you think of yourself. Walk away from a spirit of negativity and stop listening to others' bad opinions about you. People will always have opinions and judgement in regards to your past wrong doings. Their opinions about you is theirs, let it come in one ear and out the other. Other people's criticism about you won't build you but it will only lower your self-esteem. Learn to ignore it, don't pay any mind. Maintain your peace of mind and love yourself more. By doing this, you will always be blessed beyond measure, and you will continue to flourish because your mind is positive and remains clear of doubts, and negativity. As a result, you will have more energy and be more productive.

God has already forgotten all your past mistakes. He wants to bless you more in your present life and not your past experiences. But if you are still stuck in the past, it will be hard for you to accept the new blessings God has in store for you now. At one point you have to decide that life has to move on for you to experience your new found life. The key point here is to move on, forget, forgive and be very kind to yourself.

Comfort zone and fear of the unknown

Human beings are creatures of habits. For most of us, we are prone to painless and easy experiences. Comfort zone is being or doing things that are familiar to us. We progress at ease and walk steadily in what we do. Being in a comfort zone is doing the same thing over and over again. It is in our nature as human beings to tend to stick to a comfortable surroundings. Most of us tend to dislike changes and have fear of the unknown. As a result, we confine ourselves to a small area where we are more comfortable and hinder ourselves from so many good things that are happening on the outside.

For things to move forward, we have to be ready to face and learn new things. We have to be ready to challenge ourselves, get out of the comfort zone and step outside of the box to see what else is out there. We grow by accepting new challenges and push our boundaries to do what seems unfamiliar. Success normally does not come easy, it requires determination, sweat at times, and it might raise anxiety, but the Bible is telling us not to fear. And this might be a good time to raise the level of our faith in God and our belief for the unknown.

You reap what you sow

You reap what you sow is an English proverb, which means you finally *have to face up to the consequences of your own action*. This is similar to a very common proverb of "What goes around comes around." For some, they ask if it has a biblical basis – and the answer is an absolute yes, as it says in the Bible: *"For he that sows to his flesh shall of the flesh reap corruption, but he that sows to the Spirit shall of the Spirit reap life everlasting." Good produces good, and evil produces evil."*

I am not a farmer, but I know a thing or two about being a good farmer. For a farmer to experience a good harvest, they start with choosing good and healthy seeds. Once the seed is in the ground, all that's left is for a farmer to believe and have faith that the seed that he planted will eventually grow into a big crop. With care and love to the plant, by watering, feeding the soil with compost, and of course, with God's blessing of good weather, that farmer will experience a bountiful harvest. But it all starts with the choice of a good seed to plant before anything else.

Plant Good Seeds

Among the things that will increase our blessings is planting good seeds; doing good things while we are still living here on planet earth. From anyone who is very close to me, you may hear that I tend to use the word "Bless" often. I call myself blessed all the time. I call my friends and family *blessed* and I just like to wish others to be blessed. It is a new habit that I just accrued, and I think it is a good reinforcement habit. It is my strongest belief that once I bless you, you will bless me in return as well. I am not saying that I am perfect in any shape or form, though. I just recently picked up this habit and it is working wonders in my own daily life. First of all, saying that word 'bless' helps me feel good. I take delight when someone just wishes me back, saying, "Be blessed as well." The Bible is telling us to have the habit of planting the right seed. It is stated that:

> *"Do not be deceived: God cannot be mocked.*
> *Whatever a man sows, he will reap in return.*
> *The one who sows to please his flesh, from the flesh will*
> *reap destruction;*

But the one who sows to please the Spirit, from the Spirit
will reap eternal life"

Choose wisely the kind of seed you want to sow while you
have the chance to direct your course. Be careful not to
wish a bad thing to your neighbors or friends because that
is like sowing a bad seed. Hosea 10:12 says:

I said, 'Plant the good seeds of righteousness,
And you will harvest a crop of love.
Plow up the hard ground of your hearts,
For now is the time to seek the LORD,
That he may come and shower righteousness upon you.'

Being obedient to God's ways

In whatever you do, make God a priority. Make God the
center of your daily routine in your life. Don't rely on your
own understanding. God wants us to go to Him and it
pleases Him very much when He knows His children
depend on Him. As we are born made of flesh, it is very
hard to resist all the temptations in the world. I pray to
God to help us walk with Him. I am praying for the Holy
Spirit to walk with us and show us God's ways. As who
walks in Godly- like ways will experience God's abundant
blessings. Good pleases God's ways. In whatever we do, just
release it to God, and let God be the judge of everything.

I am a work in progress when it comes to being clean of all sins. I am praying to God to be more patient with me and never give up on me. I wish I could say that I am clean and without sin. All I can ask is for God to have mercy on me, for Him to look deep into my heart and never let go of my hand, and to also help me resist temptation. Yet we will fail and sin, but Christ gave His life so our SINS may be washed away in His blood.

Being impatient, having a spirit of quitting

Building a dream, acting on it, planting your seeds even with sweat and tears to the stage of reaping your harvest or reward - we call this period a **waiting time**. A waiting time is a moment in life where winners and losers are born. Most of us get tired easily. We quit fast before we see the final results of our hard work. We give up easy before we see harvest. Most people, when things get tough they become impatient and lose focus. As a tendency, we stop in the middle before reaching the finish line. And for some they quit even before they start.

A waiting time is a challenging time. I am not yet to find someone who likes to wait. By nature we are inpatient, we want to see results now. We are in a period of 'now.' Our generation is not build to wait. Abraham and Sarah waited for decades for their promise of having a child to pass.

But they waited, they waited without giving up. Ok, we see them being human eventually they messed up a bit, by taking matters into their own hands. But overall, they waited for the promise of God to pass. Jacob waited for fourteen good years before he was finally able to marry the love of his life, Rachel. Well, we know that he was deceived along the way, but he was patient, he persevered without quitting.

Over and over again, we are reminded that good things come to those who wait. Isaiah 40:31 says this, "But they who wait for the LORD shall renew their strength; they shall mount up with wings like eagles; they shall run and not be weary; they shall walk and not faint."

Who doesn't like eagles? Every time I see eagles in a sentence, I automatically think of victory, fearlessness, power, just the state of being energized. To the Native Americans, eagles have a very powerful symbolization. They consider eagles to be sacred. This is derived from the fact that they are the highest flying birds and are believed by the Natives that they were seen to fly so high near to the creator of heaven and earth. It is being stated that the eagle is the chief over all the winged creatures. They are the main symbol of great courage, wisdom, and strength.

They are here with the main purpose to carry messages to the creator.

During the waiting time, Isaiah 40:31 is giving us strong advice as to why we should wait patiently for the Lord to work his wonders within us, for those with patience will mount up with wings like eagles. Patience has its own reward. You have to come to terms with the reality that it is okay to fail and learn from your mistakes. Pick yourself up and start over again.

A waiting time is there as a test and it prepares us to be stronger for something big and grandeur from God. Having abundant blessings is not for a faint of heart. This is the time when God prepares us, hones us and molds us to be sensible, to handle His multitudes of overwhelming, over and above, overflowing blessings.

Such kind of responsibility is not for everyone. You have to be ready, well prepared, and well equipped before you can see your final rewards. In conclusion, what I am trying to say is, embrace the moments when things go horribly wrong; continue to praise God in a hallway while waiting for your doors to be opened for you. Failures and hardships are there to build our character and strengthen us. I am yet to find a successful person say that they didn't go through hardship before they reaped rewards. Most successful people have developed a sense of perseverance in them.

Being jealous and envious

Being jealous or being envious is a feeling that one develops when feeling less than, less deserving, or feeling more inadequate. It occurs when a person lacks another's possessions and superiority. In short, jealousy is a sin. Jealousy and envy to your co-worker's, neighbors' or friends' abundance, will only hinder your own blessings. God in so many ways discourages us from being envious of what does not belong to us. Instead, the Bible encourages us on building love.

The Bible emphasizes that **Love** is patient, love is kind. It does not envy, it does not boast, it is not proud. Instead of jealousy, replace it with love. Just be a person to overcome evil with blessings. Just remember that your time is coming. Instead of being jealous, I would say learn how your neighbor improved so much. Learn about the ways and the secret that lead to your friend's blessings. In most cases, if you praise your friend's success/advancement, that friend is more than likely to tell you what he/she did to reach where they are.

Most divorces have been recorded as a product of unnecessary jealousies. When a person's heart is full of jealousy, it causes that person to think irrationally. The wisdom of God normally departs from a jealous person. As a result, a jealous or envious person ends up causing more harm to his/her own self and others. Instead of being envious, develop a habit of celebrating others' development/success. This way, you are more likely to receive more of God's blessings and cause no harm to one's self.

Showing Off/hypocrites

Clearly, don't do good deeds just to show off. If you have to do good, just do it without waiting for praises or broadcasting it to the whole wide world. If you have to help a troubling neighbor, Jesus is instructing us to give/help without showing off to others because our rewarder is not the people around us. Our rewarder is God, and He sees what is being done in total privacy. Don't go seeking for credit from another human being after giving to the needy. God sees your effort and rewards you amazingly in the open.

In Matthew 6:1 says: *"Take care not to do your good deeds publicly or before men, in order to be seen by them; otherwise you will have no reward with and from your Father who is in heaven."* Here we see it is an open warning to be careful of impressing people when you give. If you have to do good for someone else, just do it without expecting praises from another person. No good deeds go in vain without God seeing it. He is the one you should always strive to impress and not human beings.

To be blunt, we see and learn that Jesus is not a fan of hypocrites at all. On Matthew 6:5 (NLT) Jesus openly told us: *"When you pray, don't be like the hypocrites who love to pray publicly on street corners and in the synagogues where everyone can see them. I tell you the truth that is all the reward they will ever get."*

Pure Laziness

This might be a self-explanatory topic, yet I am going to be frank with myself and to my readers. To some, this topic might sound a bit offensive (I hope you don't see it this way). But the truth needs to be told. We are here to help each other. We are here to build and lift each other's spirit. The goal is to better our standard of living and enjoy God's abundance to the fullest. Believe me, I am learning a lot while I am writing this book. This material in a written format enabled me to think deeper, restructure, and re-evaluate my own life. For most part, writing this book has been my self-therapy, and it's like I am discovering myself for the very first time.

While on the topic of laziness; I am going to say it exactly the way it is. Laziness does not produce fruits. Don't expect that we will move forward in life by just sitting, doing nothing, and expecting miracles. We can sit down and visualize the whole day. Pray all kind of prayers to a point of crying blood tears. We can recite all kind of prayers out there, but if we don't get up and work, trust me, nothing will mature and we will be digging ourselves a poverty hole.

To consolidate our points of discussion, I base and go back to the Bible's teachings. This line below may sound bluntly rude, but is it written and found in our very own holy scripture.

On 2 Thessalonians 3:10, "He who does not work, neither shall he eat." Ouch that hurts and cuts deep. Here, we see that the scripture didn't want to spare anyone's feeling. It simply stated that if you don't work you don't get to eat. It sounds harsh, mean, and rude, yes, but it is an honest truth. And sometimes, the truth comes wrapped in sandpaper. Honest truth can sometimes be rough and it hurts.

God is motivated and moved by hard work. Whether we are working for ourselves or for someone else, it does not matter. Hard work pays. God has said in so many Bible verses that He blesses the working hands and despises laziness. God didn't try to beat around the bush. He didn't hide his feelings or cut corners. He gave us straight like the way it is without sugar-coating anything.

Parable of the talents

A story of "Parable of the talents" also called "Parable of the Minas" comes in my mind. In the Bible, we have heard about the story of Parable of Talents in the Gospel of Matthew and also in the Gospel of Luke. They are basically similar stories told in two different places, by two different sources. The parable written in Gospel of Luke is also called the "Parable of the Pounds".

Basically, in the story of the parable of talents, we see that a master is planning a go-away trip. Before he went away, he called his three servants and entrusted them with his property. To the first servant, he gave five talents, to the second servant, he gave two talents, and to the third servant, he gave only one talent; each according to his ability. And then the master drives away to his journey. But one thing is missing here, the fact that we don't see the master explaining to them on how to use these talents, no instructions were given to them, whatsoever.

Now, the First servant who received five talents went out directly to put his money to good use. He went to put his money to work. The Bible says that he managed to produce five more times of what he had initially been given as a capital. The second servant also did similar work. He went out and produced double of what he was entrusted at the beginning. The third servant who was given only one talent has a different story. We find out that he is the laziest among the three servants. He decided that he's not going to do anything with the money. He took the money, dug a hole in the ground, and buried the money. How foolish of him. At least if he had put this money in a savings account somewhere in a bank, he would have gained interest on it. But no, this servant was so lazy to even use his mind to think. He chose the easiest way possible. We are learning here that sometimes *shortcuts and easy ways do not pay off*.

When the master returned, the first servant presented in front of him the original five talents. He did well and made five more talents, and in total, he presented ten talents to his master. The Bible says that the master was so pleased with him and said, "Well done, good and faithful servant!" The master added, "Since you have been faithful with few things, I will put you in charge of many more things."

A similar story also for the second servant who doubled his capital. The master was delighted with the second servant as well and likewise, he appointed him to be in charge of a bigger task. Now we see a third servant; it is interesting to see that most of the time, lazy people always come with their long justification as to why they fail to achieve something. This third servant came up with a long story of excuses as to why he didn't put his capital to good use. Instead, he buried the money in the ground. We see in the story that the master was so angry at him that he took back the one talent he gave him and gave that talent to the first servant who had ten.

It is interesting to me that I feel like the master knew the lazy behavior of the third servant. Thus, he entrusted him with only one talent to begin with compared to the first and second servant who had five and two respectively. I have a feeling that he received only one talent because his attitude of being lazy had long preceded him. Laziness has been his norm or behavior even before meeting his master.

Matthew 25:29-30 says:

"For the one who has will be given more, and he will have more than enough.
But the one who does not have, even what he has will be taken from him.
And throw that worthless slave into the outer darkness,
Where there will be weeping and gnashing of teeth"

This parable is a very good example of the fact that God rewards efforts and not laziness. There is a saying that the rich are getting richer and the poor are getting poorer. In other words, we can look at this as the rich are getting richer because most rich people are hardworking and disciplined individuals. They work hard, invest more, and spend less. As a result, their initial capitals keep on getting bigger and bigger every day.

On the other side for most of mediocre, average living group of people if you dig deep, you will realize that average individuals live a life of paycheck to paycheck. And with the little money that they make, they spend it all and invest nothing. And sad enough, this group of people are bigger than the group of one percent folks. Something is very wrong with the overall picture of society in general. And the truth has to be told, we need prayer. Things need to change for the better. That change can be made by starting to learn from the source. Learn how successful people think, act, and do. It is an honest truth that the well-off people behave very different from most average persons.

The good news with the current world is that we all live in a world full of information. Resources are available in most libraries, bookstores, and all over the internet. For things to change, we need mastery. For instance, if we need to learn how Oprah does in her life and what characteristics she possesses, we don't need to know Oprah in person. We can find books or the many articles written about her and start learning from the source. It is always best to learn from the best. All we need is a little effort and a small amount of research. Reading materials are out there and most of them are free.

CHAPTER EIGHT

Names have a Power

An article written by Livescience.com says that Elephants have the longest gestation period of all mammals. These gentle giants' pregnancies last for more than a year and a half. The average gestation period of an elephant is about 640 to 660 days or roughly 95 weeks. By comparison, a human being's pregnancy lasts for nine months, which is an average of 280 days or 40 weeks. And during this time of pregnancy, there are many uncomfortable changes that a woman goes through for a period of nine months. It is believed that in the time of incubation, when the baby is just in a mother's womb, a mother and a baby develop a strong bond with each other.

The process of childbirth, which is also commonly known as *labor and delivery*, is a very uncomfortable and a painful process to any woman. Whether it is through normal birth or cesarean birth, it is still a very painful and uncomfortable experience to a mother. But again, apart from the pain that a mother endures during childbirth, it is also a special moment in time when a mother and a father are given this big opportunity to unlock or open this beautiful, miraculous gift that has been entrusted to them by God Himself. Childbirth marks that special moment when the parents get to meet their baby for the first time, to see their perfect gift, and hold their baby in their arms.

Jabez's mother is like any woman who goes through the painful childbirth experience. But her case is unique in a sense that because of the agony she experienced she went on and named her precious son Jabez. The real meaning of the name Jabez is sorrow, pain, agony. The Bible tells us that she named her son Jabez due to the fact that she birthed him through terrific pain. Without being very elaborative, the Bible does not tell us what kind of pain this mother had experienced. But what we know is that it must have been an excruciatingly painful moment to the extent of giving her own son such an unfair name.

We are not sure whether the pain this mother experienced was due to childbirth itself or was due to emotional pain, or was due to something else. We don't know for sure and we won't know. I included emotional pain because the Bible talks about Jabez's mother only, and that he had his brothers. However, it does not say anything about a father. *Was she a single mother?* Did something terrible happen to his father at the time of Jabez's birth? These are questions we can keep on asking ourselves without getting any answers. All in all, we know she must have gone through a terrible time with her pregnancy and delivery time.

The main reason why I had to paint the picture of childbirth and its painful experience is the fact that despite the agony that we as women go through during pregnancy and childbirth, parents just have to be cautious on naming their newborn babies. The name we choose for our children can play a critical role for the rest of their lives. The name one carries can either bring blessings to a person or can be a big burden to that particular individual.

For most of us, a name carries a certain meaning. Normally, this meaning is of great importance to the parents/family of the child given a name. In some cultures, the process of giving a child's name is very important. In some cases, some family members and friends gather together to do a naming celebration. My first name is Janet, which is a very common name today, but I love the meaning behind it. Janet for Janet Jackson? Well, Janet means, *"God has been gracious. It is a feminine name form of John."* Thanks to my Mother for my beautiful name.

Historically and Biblically, names carry a meaning. It also tends to describe one's qualities and characteristics. God is big with names; all His names mean something according to events, circumstances, qualities, characteristics, and traits. His most famous name is God translated from the Hebrew name, which is Elohim, meaning creator of heaven and earth. Another name is El – you find El in names like Emmanuel meaning God with us, "El Shaddai" as God Almighty and "Jehovah-jireh" meaning Jehovah will provide.

God has many names, but I just gave you a glimpse of some of His names. The point is to show you that a name carries power in it. One big name that God has given us to use on a daily basis is the name 'I AM'. I AM who I AM was the name given to Moses by God to go deliver a message to Israelites who were held captives. **'I Am'** is a very powerful name since it is God's name. The name **I Am** has been given, entrusted in us to call upon the Lord in our daily language. Whenever we say I am Janet, I am healthy, I am happy, I am prosperous, we are putting ourselves in covenant with God himself. Anything that follows after I am is believed to be powerful, of Godly, and with a truth.

Now going back to Jabez, I truly empathize with him. Can you imagine every time he had to introduce himself, he had to say, I am Jabez, I am agony, I am sorrow, and I am pain? Finding out the meaning of his name depresses me already. And this man had to live with this unfair name in his whole existence. There is power in the words that we speak; through our tongue, we can speak blessing or a curse.

We are always advised to be careful on what we speak out loud using our tongues. Whatever we speak, we confirm to God/Universe that is what we want. When you say I am in pain – pain follows. I am poor and poverty rushes to be felt. As I said earlier, whenever we put next to the words **I am**, we are having an agreement with God. There is power in the name I AM. The same is believed to be true that there is ability in words that are being spoken out loud from our own mouths. Be mindful of what you speak, words have power. Our own words can bring blessings to us and the same is true that the words that we speak can bring massive destructions to our own lives. Think before you speak. Words have the potential to build or destroy. Our tongues are mightier than any swords.

No wonder the poor man Jabez felt a compelling need to go to God and cry from the very depth of his belly to release him from the agony of his own name. Our God is a very merciful God. We know in the end that God answered his request. Again, imagine the agony he had to bear every time he had to say his own name! I love the story of Jabez so much so I had to write a whole book about him. A lot can be learned from the few verses written about this man.

CHAPTER NINE

Be a person of Gratitude

I feel like sometimes God must get so tired of us complaining and crying to Him all the time. Can you imagine having a long day at work, you are tired and you come home to a nagging wife or husband, or children every day? Just think about how you'll feel. Can you imagine having to work with an ungrateful co-worker every day? The feeling you get is exhausting or draining.

Most of us Christians need to admit we pray to God and implicate that there's no other time or day. Most of our prayers are just full of begging, complaining, and just nagging. When talking to God, we only go to Him when we have issues. In good days, we seem to forget that God exists. We need to change that and not only remember God during hard times. We must go to Him with songs of thanksgiving, praises, and gratitude at all times!

"Father God, I thank You today because I had a very wonderful day. Father, I bless Your name forever because Your love is more than enough. Even though the day has been a struggle, I look around and thank you for your glory."

Just change the tone of your voice. Instead of complaining, start praising. If you have a good day, praise God and sing a song of worship. Share with Him the good news. And when you have a bad day, of course, go to God with faith and the belief that He is going to fight your battles for you. We have to tune ourselves with a melody of going to God with thanks giving attitude despite how horrible things are. There is no mountain that is too big that cannot be moved by God. We only need to go to our Father with faith and believe that He will see us through the tough times. This way, you are going to Jehovah saying, *"I am coming to you God with this giant problem, with my own humanly mind, and I don't see how this problem can be resolved, but I believe in you and I entrust in your care knowing that nothing is impossible to you, Almighty."*

If you pray such kind of prayer, you can easily see that you have identified that you have a troubling problem that you cannot solve on your own, but you are lifting God on high to iron it out. That is better than just complaining and nagging to God all the time.

Thanksgiving Holiday

We cannot talk about being a person of gratitude without touching and talking about a Thanksgiving holiday and The feast of Tabernacle. In America and Canada, the holiday of Thanksgiving is glory, a sincerest gratitude that we receive in terms of harvest and all the blessings we have received throughout the year. In other places of the world, Thanksgiving holiday is well- known as a festival Holiday.

The same is said to a Jewish holiday called "The Feast of Tabernacle" wherein during The Feast of Tabernacle or Sukkot, Jewish people convene in Jerusalem to remember and thank God for His provision while in the wilderness. All the people from the cities, including the Gentiles, are gathered in the city of Jerusalem to praise and worship God. Both of these holidays mark the time of celebrating life and thanking God for the blessings of harvest and God's life provision.

We are biblically instructed to be more than persons of gratitude. We are instructed to be persons of Thanksgiving in everything that is provided to us. Create a life of purposely praising God and thanking God at all times. As in 1 Thessalonians 5:18, the Bible says:

> *"In everything give thanks;*
> *for this is God's will for you in Christ Jesus."*

To fully complete this chapter, I feel the need to look at some of the habits and characteristics of most grateful individuals. This will help us understand better our topic of being persons with gratitude and thanksgiving. There are so many benefits that one gets by living a life of gratitude. Here, we will look at some of the traits that grateful people have. In other words, we are trying to see how we can benefit by being more grateful as opposed to living a life without purpose and ungratefulness.

Happiness

We all want to be happy and live a life full of happiness. In today's world, people are spending a considerable amount of money on books and self-help materials on how to be happy again. We see that case, especially in developed countries, where the number of depressed people is increasing at an alarming rate. We live a fast-paced life, chasing every dollar. As a result, most people are lonely and very unhappy. And yet, we are being told that the act of living a happy life is an individual's state of mind.

Life can be unfair; life can pass by really fast. Don't let circumstances overwhelm you. Find something that will work for you. If you feel like staying in the house alone, depressed and sorrowful, you'd better step outside the house. Go for a walk in the park or choose to do something that will lift your spirit up. You cannot change how the world reacts, but you can start by changing how you behave and react to the unhappy environment. Hence, happiness is a choice. No one is in charge of your own happiness except you. Decide to take charge of your own happiness. Don't be happy because of other people or the mundane, material things, this type of happiness will not last. Be happy and content with your current circumstances. Be grateful for what you have now, big or small. Be happy with yourself. God did not create a bad person, and to judge ourselves or someone else as not measuring up is saying God made a mistake with you. God does not make mistakes.

Grateful people appear to be happier in life and are more satisfied with what they have in front of them. Life's challenges don't seem to shake them off. They walk a life full of anticipation. They expect for better things to happen in every objective. When your life is full of happiness, you normally tend to remove all the bad impurities and toxicity from your inner mental state. You tend not to hold grudges and forgive more, but know when to remove yourself from things or people that can play on your mental state. This is so important.

I have a friend whose husband left after 35 years of marriage. She became angry with God. Why would he allow this to happen? She voiced strongly to her pastor she wanted a miracle to bring him back. Her pastor took her hands in his and said, "You may not like what I am about to say, but maybe this is your miracle." And he was right. Her faith was able to grow without the negative remarks from her husband, and so her happiness also grew. Her daily walk is one of trust and thankfulness now.

Grateful people are positive thinkers

Grateful individuals tend to be positive thinkers: Positive thinkers are people who purposely choose to see the world from a bright side, but this does not mean that they don't see all the negativity of today. But by living a life of choices, they face every problem with a corresponding solution. When you think this way, you tend to have hope and face life with a great anticipation. Positive thinkers are more settled, calmer individuals with clear judgments.

While on the other side, people who think negatively normally magnify their problems to the point that they cannot even see how their problems are going to be resolved. Negative people are complainers, appearing to be weak. They tend to view life unfairly, and in most cases, they achieve very little in life. Rarely, is anything seen as their faults.

Positive thinkers tend to focus their mind and energy on positive outcomes rather than on negative results. They always see a light at the end of every tunnel. It is easy to have great faith in God if you are a positive thinker. Because as we already know, faith is believing the unseen. This is how the positive thinkers believe that things are not that bad. No matter how big the problem is at the end of the day, there is a solution. It is easier for a positive individual to magnify God than a problem. The same is true that it is even easier for an optimistic person to be a good believer of God. Positive people live a life of awareness about what is going on around them. And so it is often easier to hang around with positive thinkers than negative individuals. They are also more likable by their peers.

Negative people can easily drain others because most of the time, they face life as victims, and tend to see and treat things unfairly. They also tend to have poor judgments and make decisions unwisely. Their rationale is always off- key. If you are a positive thinker, you will most definitely enjoy life more than a person with a negative mindset.

A Grateful person lives a life full of purpose and hope

Grateful people tend to be more confident with themselves. They know who they are, and that they are the children of the highest and only true God. Small issues in life don't faze them because they know that they are saved by God, nothing is impossible. *"For with man it is not possible but for God, all things are possible."* Matthew 19:26. Even through the tough and rough patches of life, there is always a light at the end of the tunnel. Our faith is really tested during the tough times. It is even harder to be grateful and be thankful to God when everything seems to be going wrong. But we are being encouraged not to rely on our own understanding, but with God's wisdom. Grateful personalities tend to focus more on the positive side of life rather than problems that they are facing because to them; life has a meaning and a purpose.

They are satisfied in the present moment

Being satisfied in the present state does not mean that you don't dream for the future to change. It means that you are content and grateful with whatever God has given you now but again, you are living a life of peace and joy knowing that more and better things are coming your way. It is also believed that God blesses us more when we tend to be more grateful to small things we get at the moment rather than waiting to be grateful when we have more tomorrow. By not being grateful with little that you have now, you are more likely to be ungrateful even when you obtain what you desire. The past is past, tomorrow is not promised, live your life serving God today, and feel good about you.

Develop a spirit of being grateful for what you have. Look around you and find a reason to be purposely grateful. You have had a full meal today, be grateful for that. You have a job. You have a family. Be grateful for the fresh air that you get to breathe. Be grateful to God for having a roof over your head. It does not matter whether that roof is just a shed of a patch of grass, it is a roof to keep you dry from rain, so be grateful anyway. By doing this now, God will eventually be able to provide you with more than what you currently have.

Make God feel compelling that if Janet is grateful for the small things, I might as well provide her with more. Janet is grateful with this small house, but her dream is to have a bigger and better house. At this point, as Janet, I will need to do something for God to accomplish this, so that I can feel good about the hard work that I have put in. God only knows what is truly best for us. That is, when God puts his angels to work for you, your complete life status will start moving towards accommodating you to have your dream house. This is when you start experiencing instant changes over the sudden blessings in every area of your life. If you have a job, you will see that your salary at work can be increased, or God will find a way for you to be removed from your current job to a different and better job. He will sometimes close one door and open a new one. If you are a business person, you will see that your sales are starting to skyrocket; things are moving in the right direction to accommodate this shift. As a result, your income will be doubled or tripled and eventually, you will be in a position to afford your dream house. That is what we call the *Divine powers of God*. Be grateful for where you are planted today for God to be able to move you to a land of milk and honey. Start being grateful today for you to land in your wishful destination area tomorrow. Be grateful, hardworking, and have patience. All in God's time.

CHAPTER TEN

Generational Legacy

I had to include this chapter simply because I want us to understand that when gaining God's blessing, we are going to gain the blessings not just for us but for many generations to come. Legacy can mean inheritance, birthright, and heritage. It is something that has been passed down by ancestors. I am praying to God that you are going to be that person who changes not only your life, but also the lives of so many other generations to come. I am not here to dream small dreams with you. We are going to dream and shoot for high dreams. We are going to be the change that is needed in our families, our children, and their children to come. Why can't we decide to be that change today?

You have to realize that when God blesses us, He goes over and above. He does not think small. When He blessed Abraham, He promised to bless Him and His many descendants to come. When God decides to bless you, He goes bananas. He pours blessings to us that we cannot contain. We are the children of the highest God. If you expect small, even the results you will receive are going to be small. Enlarge your borders today and be cautious not to put God in a limitation Box.

The generational blessing is a very biblical concept that God has shown to us in many ways. In Proverbs 13:22, God says, "A good man leaves an inheritance to his Children's children."

You have seen before in this book also that I have prayed to the God of Abraham, Isaac, and Jacob – I did this purposely because I knew that I am coming down to this chapter to talk about the topic of leaving a legacy to our children.

By now, we all have prayed and understood the prayer of Jabez. Despite the fact that the prayer of Jabez said *bless me indeed*, using a lot of the word *'me'*, it does not mean that we are praying for just us, neither does it mean that I am praying just for my own benefits. Today, we are praying for God to bless us and we are going to be the individuals who will pass the blessings down to our children and their children. Because of the prayer, we are praying today that our children and their children will not have to suffer. Our children and their children will benefit from the fact that we prayed and cried to a living God. You made that change possible and it starts within and from you, as you allow God to reside in you and guide you.

Abraham, Isaac, and Jacob are the three generations that have tremendously benefited from God's abundant generational legacy. In short, this tells us that the same God who was there during the time of Abraham is the same God who blessed Isaac and the same blessings were passed down to Jacob. In fact, if we decide to keep going down, you will find Joseph the son of Jacob, who was also blessed beyond measure despite all the life's challenges that he encountered. Starting from being sold into slavery, he was thrown in jail. Later on, we learned that God remembered Joseph and lifted him so high until he became a country leader in a foreign land of Egypt. The agreement that Abraham made with God so many years ago made way for Joseph to experience God's favor. This is a proof that when God blesses you,

He blesses you and your generations to come. I want us to be that change. Decide today to be the one to leave that generational legacy.

In 2 Timothy 1-5 God says that "I am reminded of your sincere faith, a faith that dwelt first in your grandmother Lois and your mother Eunice and now, I am sure dwells in you as well"

This verse reminds me of my own life in so many ways. You see I am who I am today because my grandparents prayed for me. I have to keep this momentum going. I am one of the luckiest to have my ancestors who prayed for me, others have never been lucky in this sense. But if you are reading this book and if you are one of the people who cannot name any person who prayed for you, then this message is for you. I want you to be that change. You start today by praying for your children and their children's children and let them know you are praying for them. Choose to be the change that is needed in your family and your generations to come. Set the standard for others to follow. I feel blessed because the standard was already set for me by my grandparents and my mother. But that does not mean that since my grandparents prayed, I don't need to pray anymore. It is still my sole priority to keep this legacy going, for others and myself.

For some, they will have doubt and may not be able to envision as to how they can be that change or as to how they can make an impact for other generations to come. I am here to encourage you today to believe in the power that is within you. Have faith in the work of the Lord as faith is to believe all that is unseen. Just pray and believe. Leave it to God to make His wonders come to past. Be encouraged that when it is time for you to leave this world, you leave a mark that you were once on the planet earth. Leave a mark that will have an impact not only for one generation but three generations deep and even more. Leave a generation legacy.

One of the best examples of wanting to leave a legacy is Sam Walton. He was an American businessman and entrepreneur best known for finding the retailers Walmart and Sam's Club. He died in 1992 at a very young age of 74 years old. He wrote a book titled, *"Made in America,"* his true life story. This book is one of my favorite books. He wrote this book while he was in his sickbed during his last days. You have to read it to understand how he persevered to rise to such high grounds. In his self-portrait, he talked about the ambition, inspiration, heart, optimism, and of course, leaving a legacy. It is hard for me to summarize all of the remarkable work he did here, you have to read to understand it. Sam Walton died two decades ago now, but his name still lives with us today. To be frank, I don't see the end of Walmart. Walmart today has become the landmark of America. His children and other people in many generations to come will always enjoy the fruits of his hard labor, dedication, and his love for his family. Talking about leaving a legacy, Sam Walton's surely left his footprints. His principles and achievements have become immortal and are going to be remembered and continue to touch so many people from generation to generation, even if all don't agree with his principles.

We are all not going to be on the same level as Sam Walton or may not want to be. And of course, leaving a legacy does not necessarily need to be in a monetary form. When we talk about leaving a legacy, we are talking about you leaving back something of value. Let people miss you, remember you when you are long gone. Let your beloved ones see the gap of your departure. The idea behind this is having the desired need to be remembered for all the good things that you have contributed to this world.

Leaving a legacy does not necessarily be of money and fortunes. There are so many ways one can decide to leave behind as a legacy and it does not cost much. Love and time are among those things. Anyone can afford to leave a gift of love and time. Most people will remember the memories and presence more than anything. Love and time are gifts that both rich and poor can give to their spouses, children, friends, and colleagues. Most legacies remembered are in a form of service to humanity. Create a life story where your purpose is living a life for others.

The other form of leaving a legacy is through being a mentor. A mentor is a person who is regarded as a more experienced or more knowledgeable individual within an area of expertise. This will involve giving guidance, role modeling, personal development and giving support to others with less experience.

For me, growing up, that person will be my uncle Michael Simwaba. I grew up without a father. Uncle Michael, who is a very good English teacher, stepped up to the plate and took over the role of a father figure, mentor, life supporter and a guardian angel. He saw something remarkable in me at a very young age. He believed in me even before I was able to see the value in me.

My mom's small family lived in a two-bedroom, government self-contained cottage. The house was located up the greenish Jacaranda Hill. I remember standing by a window seeing my uncle walking up this steep rough road of the hill, coming to see me at our house. He must have walked up this hill at least three times a week or even more. This was after a long day of working with students at his high school where he was teaching. My uncle would come and sit down with me to read books such as "Things fall apart", "No Longer at Ease" by Chinua Achebe. We must have read these books from cover to cover at least twice. I was a young girl then and till now, I feel these memories, the special kind of relationships we shared, will last a lifetime in my brain.

Uncle Michael if you are reading this book, I just want to say thank you so much for dedicating your time and love to shaping me into the woman I am today. People like you are good examples of people who bring positive change into this world. For that, I love you so much and I am forever grateful.

"Carve your name on hearts, not tombstones. A legacy is etched into the minds of others and the stories they share about you." — Shannon L. Alder.

CHAPTER ELEVEN

Main Points

"Oh, that you will BLESS ME INDEED.
And ENLARGE MY BORDERS.
And that your HAND MIGHT BE with me.
And you will keep me from evil so that
it might not hurt me!

Some people will argue that this is not the best prayer because it is so self-centered and selfish. In his whole prayer, in almost every line, Jabez has used the term *me*, and *my*. He just prayed for himself. He didn't pray for others, for his family, or even for his wife. If he had one, we don't know for sure. All we know is that he had a mother who gave him an awful name and that he had his brothers. We know about him having siblings because the Bible says that Jabez was more honorable than his brothers. The Bible does not say if he had a father because the father is not mentioned anywhere. We can say for sure that this prayer is really self-centered since Jabez just prayed for God to bless only him and not any other individual.

If you view this prayer as a self-centered prayer, you are very right, and I am right there with you. I am with you because all my life I was taught to pray differently. I was not taught to pray like Jabez. But now, I am so glad I came across this prayer because it has taught me a big lesson that it is okay to be self-centered, to be selfish at times and to pray for me, myself and I without even feeling guilty or ashamed. Especially if my blessings positively influence others.

A Prayer Closet

In Matthew 6:6, as part of the Sermon on the Mount; Jesus is instructing and showing us the importance of praying in total privacy. Hence, I call it "A Prayer Closet." Jesus is telling us the importance of praying in the environment of stillness, quietness, without any distraction between you and God. Matthew 6:6 says: *"But when you pray, go into your most private room. Close the door, pray to your Father who is in secret; and your Father, who sees in secret, will reward you in the open."*

I want you to ask yourself this one big question: If you don't pray for yourself, who do you think will pray for you? Who do you think will be best to present your needs to God than yourself? You are the only one who knows all that is going on in your life. You know all the good, the bad and ugly issues that surround you; the darkness in your life, the sins that you have committed as a human being; sometimes you have committed sins that are so dark you cannot even tell your father or mother, or your pastor. But I bet that when you are all alone in your own closed private prayer room, you are more than likely to tell God 100% truth when it is just you and God alone. You and God know your life's challenges better than anyone else. I read this quote on a blog: "You are who you really are, when no one is looking."

I am blessed to be a blessing
"God, I pray today that you will BLESS me indeed
so that I can be a blessing to so many other people."
In Jesus Name Amen.

If you have ever traveled on a plane, the air hostess gives some instructions before the plane takes off. He or she will tell you that in case of an emergency, it is advised that you put the oxygen mask on yourself first before you start attending to someone else. To make it more understandable, in some planes, they will show you a picture of a baby sitting next to you – and you are advised that you have to attend to your needs first before you attend to your child next to you. This is a good example of being a good selfish and a good self-centered individual. The main reason is, if there is an emergency, and if you are well equipped, you will be in a much better position to help others. The same goes for blessings – if you are well blessed, it will be easy for you to bless others. I pray today that God will find favor in us and bless us greatly so that we can be a blessing to others. We call ourselves blessed today in faith that we are blessed indeed and that God has found favor in us.

Blessed Hands

Furthermore, I would like to accentuate that I am not saying that praying like Jabez is the only right way to pray. I am not saying that if you just pray like Jabez today and tomorrow you will be rich and all of your issues will go away. But what I know for a fact is that praying the right prayer to God will absolutely get God's attention. When Jesus *says yes to your prayer, nobody can say no, as this is one of my favorite song by Michelle William.* All you need to move forward is a BIG YES from God. Luke 1:37

says, "For with God nothing shall be impossible." A big Yes from God plus a hard working spirit equals over and above abundant success. The key to any man's success is God's approval, which is all we need in anything we do. The enemy cannot put a curse on what God has already blessed.

Proverb 16:3
Says: "Commit to the Lord whatever you do and he will establish your plans."
As well in Jeremiah 29:11: "For I know the plan I have for you," declares the Lord, "Plans to prosper you and not to harm you. Plans to give you HOPE and a future."
A future of abundant living.

For the blessings to take place, for the blessings to mature, you have to do your part. You have to do something. You have to take action. In other words, you have to work for it. Even a person who wins a lottery took action first by getting up from a lazy chair and going to a nearby gas station to buy a lottery ticket. You cannot win on a lottery ticket if you didn't buy one. You have to actually work/ act upon your wishes to come true. Don't just sit and expect that you will receive over and above blessings that you don't deserve. There are so many teachings in the Bible in which God blesses the work of our hands... This tells us how eager our gracious Father wishes us well. He wants to see us flourishing. He takes pride and joy when He sees His children flourishing in Him and not worried at all times.

Proverb 14:23 says:
"All Hard work brings a profit
but mere talk leads only to poverty."

Should I say more? The scripture above is just one of the examples wherein God is instilling in us the attitude to work for our blessing. In Genesis 2:3, God worked hard for six days while He was creating this world and all of us in it. He took the pleasure of enjoying His creation and all the work that He had done and on the seventh day, He rested. Hard work is something that God seeks in us. I cannot sit here today with a straight face and tell you that if you pray like Jabez you will definitely be blessed. You have to give God something to bless; Give God reasons as to why He wants to bless you.

God rewards our efforts. God rewards all kind of efforts, whether they are big or small. God wants to multiply your effort – give Him something to multiply. You have to plant a good seed first for a seed to multiply. Even something as small as that mustard seed I mentioned earlier in the book.

Proverb 12:11 says:
"Those who work their land will have abundant food,
But those who chase fantasies have no sense."

The teachings of the Lord about good work ethics are everywhere in the Bible.

I really like this verse below, and I am praying to God to help me try to apply it in my daily work.

Titus 2:7-8 says:
"In everything set them an example by doing what is good.
In your teaching show integrity, seriousness and soundness
of speech that cannot be condemned, so that those who
oppose you may be ashamed because they have nothing
bad to say about us."

This sounds to me like a mission statement, and hands down, this can make the best mission statement more than most of the mission statements out there.

In every job that you hold big or small, whether it is a paying job or just internship, whether it is your own company or your own business, dream job or just a temporary job, you should always strive to set yourself apart from the crowd. Try to stand out. Titus is telling us to give our best, work hard, and work hard even when people are not looking. This kind of attitude will come to the rescue when an enemy is threatening your life. You know the devil is a liar, and it will come a day he will try you – be ready to put him in shame.

This kind of habit opens many God's blessings to your reputations as a hard worker and an honest person. It will precede you and define your character. Also, it is with this kind of attitude where you see that God blesses people over and above what they can even dream. Have you ever just wondered why some people's lives seem to look like they are just flourishing? If you look deep, they all have similar traits– they work hard, they are disciplined, they are careful, they invest and spend less, and they carefully calculate every move they make and for most part they are givers. And God is moved by them and He keeps on showering them with abundant blessings. He keeps multiplying the fruits of their labor. And today, this is the kind of blessings that I pray we will all experience in our daily lives, in Jesus name. Amen

Wait With Expectancy

While we are taking action on our God-given dreams and also persistently praying for God to bless the work of our hands, it is crucial that we wait. Wait with patience and wait with great expectations. And it is a known fact that during the waiting period, we grow stronger and mature. It is during this waiting period in which it is said that God does a wonderful work in us. He is building us and making us ready to handle the blessings that are waiting ahead of us.

We also have to bear in mind that it is during this waiting period that our patience is being tested. This is the time when the devil will test us, and he will want us to quit and fall. This stage sets apart the winners and losers. The weak cannot handle living in a waiting period. I am a living proof that God's timing is always the best. Wait with patience and expectation and that God will act upon your wishes.

While you are in a waiting period, think positively and believe with your whole heart that your prayers have been answered. It does not hurt to think positive, does it? I read somewhere and I am in total agreement with the statement *that it takes the same amount of energy to think positively as when you think negatively.* God's word tells us that if you diligently work hard, wait with great expectations and have faith in Him, you will yield good results.

Principles of life

We live a life of principles. For the sake of our reading, I have come up with a principle that will help you tap into the abundance of God's blessings. There are very many other principles to follow out there. And this one version is the summary of all that we have learned so far concluded from the main key points written in this book.

To be fully successful and to enjoy the favors of God's blessings, you will need to follow certain guidance or principles of life. You will need to develop some sort of life discipline. Life can be hard if you make it hard, but life is very simple if you follow the invisible laws and principles that govern our daily lives. In short be good, act good, and observe God's ways. You will surely do fine and live a blessed life of richness that God has orchestrated for you to have.

"Bless Me Indeed" steps and Principles.

1. => Observe your needs - Dream
(Have a Clear Vision of what you want to change/or what you want to pray about. Dream a big dream)

2. => Bring your needs to God's attention
    (Pray – Pray alone or in a group of people -it does not
    matter – Just Pray to the right God; The Living God,
    God of Israel–call upon God to create holy grounds.)

3. => Work Hard/work diligently on whatever goal you
    want to achieve
            (Take action, it is okay to dream but again,
                    act upon the dream)

4. => Have faith in God and be obedient to His ways
    (Faith believes in the unknown. Faith, Believing, and
    Obedience are three secrets to get God's attention.)

5. => Develop a spirit of Giving – Give and Tithe
    (Tithing is the act of giving God what is righteously His.)

6. => Wait patiently with great expectations
    (Believe that God is going to act. Don't Lose Hope while
    waiting for God's answer. Have patience while waiting.)

With a Positive attitude, know and affirm that God will
grant your request. I guarantee you that God will have no
choice other than opening up the windows of heaven and
pouring out to you, blessings that will overflow.

IN CONCLUSION

"PRAYER OF JABEZ"

The prayer of Jabez might be one of the shortest stories ever written in the Bible. But it is one story that is believed to be filled with Godly divine powers. It is one of a kind prayer that is so powerful if applied correctly and diligently, it can literally transform one's life. There are so many documented stories written as to how people's lives have been transformed by this very prayer. One of the best example will be Bruce Wilkinson. He is highly documented on how blessed he was by just introducing us to this story of Jabez. It was said that he became a household name with his publication of The Prayer of Jabez. His book was among the fastest-selling books.

The Prayer of Jabez is very fascinating to me in a sense that out of only two verses, one can learn so much and be empowered about the ways of life. Every chapter that is written in this book is in one way or another, whereas the materials have been captivated around the very same prayer. Some of the topics that we have covered are topics like obedience and fear for one true God, blessings, abundance, favor, divine protection, the meaning of one's name, the power of Forgiveness, Life's Legacy, and the power of tongue and of words that we speak. All these powerful topics are embedded in this one short prayer – "PRAYER OF JABEZ".

The Prayer of Jabez is designed for all people from all walks of life. It is a prayer for poor or for very rich. It is a universal prayer in a sense that it is applicable to all of us regardless of religion, gender, age, education, culture and background, social status or education level. I personally apply the prayer of Jabez in almost everything. I pray a prayer of Jabez over my health, finances, family, love life, work, etc. I pray daily for God to bless me indeed, enlarge, expand, enrich, and give me his divine protection. And it works.

I have been personally blessed by the work of this book. A dream worked hard toward making it happen, God's guidance a heartfelt gift, and the feeling of pride and accomplishment. Writing this book has been my way to empower you of God's news. I, therefore, argue you to do the same and share this good news with others. Share the message of this book with your friends, family members, associates, and colleagues. Consider getting this book as a gift for them.

Let it be in your commitment to tell at least one person about this life changing theory. Good news is always worth sharing, and by sharing, not only will you be enriching someone with the Bible's powerful prayer, but you will also be blessing them. As a return, you will be blessed as well beyond your wildest dreams. I challenge you to pay it forward. For there are no good deeds that go in vain in God's eyes. We don't always see the blessing realized by another, but they are there. God works in powerful and mysterious ways. Have faith, do good, be the footsteps that someone else wants to walk in. May you be Blessed Indeed by God's grace.

In closing, Let us pray

Father God, we come to You with humble hearts and songs of praise. We say 'thank You' God because You have heard our prayers and seen our tears. We say thank You because You have chosen us to be blessed today so that we can be a blessing to others. We will continue to praise You for the work of our hands and waiting in faith with big expectations that you have answered our prayers. We are guided by positive attitudes that everything we do will yield fruits because our work has been blessed by Your hands. We pray for Your protection over us and our families. In sickness and in health, we choose today to worship You and only You, oh God of Israel.

In Jesus Name we pray, Amen.

ABOUT THE AUTHOR

Janet Kisyombe is the main advocate of living a dream life –
Her life is filled with stories from poverty to prosperity
all because of God's grace. She believes that the power to
change one's life for the better lies within our own minds.

She grew up in a rural area in Tanzania, East Africa. The
seed of Love and fear for God was well planted by her
beloved late grandparents, and also the same credit goes to
her single mother, Dr. Victoria Kisyombe. Her childhood
memories while living with her grandparents are filled
with love, joy, and full of God's wisdom.

Today, Janet resides in Owings Mills, Maryland, USA.
She works as a Clinical Manager – Facility Administrator

at the third largest dialysis company in the USA. The book of Jabez has brought supernatural Blessings to so many people, she and others have shared it with. The author believes that today is your day to experience God's abundant blessings.